The Rising Stars
Guide for
Show Biz Kids
and Their Parents

The
RISING STARS
GUIDE
for
Show Biz
Kids
and Their Parents

DAVID MATIS

Prince Paperbacks
New York

Appearing on the cover: Dominique Browder, Kellen Hathaway, John Webb, Eric Bell, Sara Teitell, Chance Carroll, Thomas Papp, Samantha Toy, Lindsay Whitney Barry, Eric Strenger, Keith Strenger, K. C. Corkery, Tristan Hathaway, Katie Fogal, Josiah Berryhill, Ali Goldman, Katrina Johnson, Alex Goldman, Carolyn Ho, Branden Zamel, Kasey O'Brien, Kelly O'Brien, and Christine Porter.

A Prince Paperback book. Published by Crown Publishers, Inc., 201 East 50th Street, New York, New York 10022. Member of the Crown Publishing Group. Random House, Inc. New York, Toronto, London, Sydney, Auckland

Prince Paperbacks and colophon are trademarks of Crown Publishers, Inc.

Manufactured in the United States of America

Library of Congress Cataloging-in-Publication Data
Matis, David.
    The Rising Stars guide for show biz kids and their parents / David Matis. — 1st ed. Includes index.
    1. Acting for television—Vocational guidance.   2. Children as actors.   3. Television advertising.   I. Rising Stars (Firm)
II. Title.
PN1992.8.A3M38   1992
791.45'0293'083—dc20   92-16445
                                                                CIP
                              ISBN 0-517-88030-X
                              1 3 5 7 9 10 8 6 4 2
                              First Edition

To my wife, Joan,
for her support,
enthusiasm, and wonderful smile.

ACKNOWLEDGMENTS

I would like to acknowledge and say thanks to the Screen Actors Guild for their assistance, and to the many fine agents and young actors with whom I have had the pleasure of working. Special thanks to Stephanie, Joy, J.J., Joyce, Jody, Bonnie, Susan, Kathy, and Eileen.

CONTENTS

Author's Note

You will notice that throughout the book, I use the pronoun *he* when referring to one child. I do so only for convenience. It's easier to stick to one pronoun. And I'd rather not invent a pronoun like *he/she* that would cover all the bases.

My choice of gender is not intended to exclude anyone. Every reference to *he* is intended to include *she*.

INTRODUCTION

Act One: Scene One

FADE IN . . . Interior Shot

You're sitting at home watching your favorite program on TV. So far, the story has been enjoyable. It's predictable, but you've had a few laughs. Then, out of the blue, one of the main characters is suddenly confronted with a problem involving (choose one of the following): a zany next-door neighbor, a plumber with an attitude, a grouchy boss, or an angry ex-spouse. Uh-oh, a real situation has developed; an unexpected twist in the plot. This is getting exciting now. How in the world will this be resolved, you wonder.

But, first . . . a few (?) words from the sponsors.

Oh no, you complain silently to yourself, they always do this at the most interesting part. Time for a quick trip to the kitchen. Your hand automatically reaches for the remote control. Quick as an Old West gunfighter, you raise the remote, take aim, and begin to press the mute button. That's when you notice the scene on your TV; it's a little boy sitting alone at a kitchen table happily eating a large bowl of cereal. Why, isn't he just the cutest little tyke, you're thinking. And look, that girl who just came into the kitchen must be his older sister and she's teasing him about his choice of cereals. He doesn't seem to mind though; look at him shovel it in. Wait a minute! She just took a bite herself. And look at the smile on her face. Now she's pouring her own bowl. The two of them are munching away together. Must be good cereal.

That commercial ends and is immediately followed by another. This time, your thumb follows through and hits the mute button. Who wants to hear a singing cockroach anyway? There's still another minute or so before the show returns, and you've forgotten about that snack in the kitchen, so you sit back and wait. And out of nowhere, this thought drops into your head: Hmmmm, that sure was a cute commercial. Wouldn't it be great if my kids could be on TV? It doesn't look all that difficult. Besides, my kids are as cute as any I've seen on the tube. And didn't the guy at the dry cleaners say that Johnny was a real character and should be on TV? And didn't Linda's teacher say she showed real talent in the junior high school play and could follow directions well? And didn't Lindsey win the Most Photogenic Award at the Town and Country Mall Beauty Contest? Yeah, I think I'll look into it. This could be a lot of fun and . . . (pause, thinking, furrowed brow), "Gee, where do I start and what am I supposed to do," you say.

End Scene One
FADE OUT

Does that little episode in front of the TV sound familiar? If so, that's not surprising. It's a variation of a scene that takes place day in and day out all across this country. Mom and Dad suddenly think, If those kids I see on TV can do that, why can't mine? Or little Samantha or Eric turns to you one evening with an excited look and says, "Mom, I want to be on TV too; just like those other kids." And why not? It sure seems like a great idea. But then the questions begin, often followed by the wrong answers or no answers at all. Then maybe you hear a few negative rumors and before you know it, an idea that seemed exciting and a lot of fun stops dead in its tracks.

But it doesn't have to turn out that way. You really may be right when you say, "My child can do that." All types of children, from babies to teenagers, are in constant demand in this interesting and lucrative business. Each year, thousands of children work in commercials, promoting everything from diapers to hamburgers. They're seen in television series, feature-length films, and movies made for TV. They even have their own talk shows and game shows. It's a great opportunity for those involved, not only to earn some money but also to have a lot of fun. Many children do quite well financially, securing enough money to pay for private school and college, and, with wise investing, have an earned income for many years later.

But not to be overlooked is the experience itself: travel, new friends, and meeting interesting people; something shared together as a family, pleasant memories and adventures to fill a scrapbook to be cherished a lifetime.

But how do you begin? How do you know if your child really has what it takes? How much time is involved? Will it cost anything? What about school? What *are* the answers to those questions?

That's what this book is about: ANSWERS! Not to confuse

you or run you around in circles, but to provide you with clear, concise information that will be helpful in beginning your child in this business. It is written with *you,* the parent, in mind; to help you understand an often confusing and crazy business, to separate the myths from the facts. You will receive complete step-by-step instructions, simple and direct, not only to put you on the right path but also to help you remain there. Included are numerous tips covering everything from auditions to contracts to photo sessions—the knowledge you will need on a day-to-day basis and which could lead to a long and successful career for your child.

Good luck and let's get started!

**The Rising Stars
Guide for
Show Biz Kids
and Their Parents**

1

COMMERCIALS, MOVIES, TELEVISION SERIES

The term Entertainment Business covers a lot of ground. It is more than the Hollywood sign and the famous "Lights, Camera, Action." It is the circus, the stage, and the stand-up comedian. It is the street juggler and musician performing for change, and some would say it probably includes most of professional wrestling. Entertainment can be hilarious, intriguing, spontaneous, and deceitful—often in the same moment. It may be controversial or dull and sometimes, for those who work within its large boundaries, even a little crazy. It means different things to different people. Many actors do not consider doing commercials as a legitimate form of their profession; others see little difference between playing one role in a commercial and a similar one in a feature film. Some people purposely work in only one specific field. Others are open to all options.

This book will not join in that argument. For simplicity's sake, all forms of work available for children in this field, including commercials, movies, television programs, print modeling, voice-overs, educational films, industrial films, and plays will fall under the headings of Show Business, Entertainment Business, The Business, or The Industry. They are, in a sense, all related. Each has a purpose to project ideas, concepts, attitudes, emotions, stories, and information to an audience—with the desire for those things to be understood. Commercials certainly have been known to entertain, inform, and move an audience just as a feature film might. To do this, producers, writers, directors, actors, production crews, and assisting personnel are all needed. The methods and final results of the commercial may indeed be different from those of a feature film, but they hold enough in common.

This book will focus primarily on commercials: getting an agent, doing auditions, shooting the job, etc. But that does not mean the other areas are excluded or should not be considered. It is simply a place to begin—a common ground. The basic information here can be applied across the board. Specific details and differences will be noted as needed.

A rule of thumb is for young actors to begin their careers in commercials, gain confidence and ability, and gradually move into auditioning for theatrical roles—small parts, a few lines here and there. The kids talented enough to read for the starring role in a motion picture or new television series have usually been around for a while. Everyone pays his dues.

Generally speaking, there are many more opportunities in commercials, especially for the beginners. The number of new commercials filmed each year far exceeds the number of new motion pictures and television shows. Another bonus is that you are not as limited by where you live. Commercials are produced in many cities all across the United States, so that means those of you not living in Los Angeles or New York still have the opportunity to pursue this. Of course, motion pictures are also filmed all across the country, and filmmakers frequently hire actors in the immediate areas of where they are working.

Throughout the book, references will be made as to which rules and regulations and other points are important to check in your local area, and how to do so. For instance, the number of hours a minor may work and what time of day that minor may begin work will vary from state to state.

Also provided in the book is a list of the regional union offices for the Screen Actors Guild (SAG) and the American Federation of Television and Radio Artists (AFTRA). These offices will be able to provide you with current listings of union-affiliated talent agencies in your area. If any of the phone numbers or addresses have been changed since the publication of this book, you should contact the union head-quarters in Los Angeles or New York for current information.

The work referred to in this book pertains primarily to union jobs—SAG and AFTRA. The majority of all commercials seen on TV, especially major spots playing to a national audience, are filmed under union contract. The majority of all roles cast in television programs and motion pictures are union. Nonunion jobs are, in most cases, lower-budget productions. They do not have to adhere to the strict union rules regarding working and auditioning or any particular pay scale or overtime hours, and are not under any obligation to provide certain amenities—such as a catered lunch on location. They do, however, have to abide by all *state* rules and regulations governing the employment of minors.

2

QUESTIONS, QUESTIONS, QUESTIONS

A few of the questions most often asked by parents before starting are: How will this business affect my child? Will he still be able to have a normal childhood? What about school? Will this cost a lot of money? What about rejection? These are certainly valid questions and should be answered.

It's true that a certain amount of time and commitment is necessary, but in many ways working in commercials is an activity like any other. For the average child, you could probably put in more time at Little League or gymnastics. Auditions generally do not take that much time (excluding the driving). When the children are working, they will usually only spend a day or two on the set. Then it's back to the normal routine. When school is in session, all auditions are after school. If children are working during school hours, a certified teacher with valid and current credentials is provided and the necessary schoolwork is done right there. More on this in later chapters.

If you're worried about the kid being spoiled or turning into a stage brat, well, there's no denying that most of the kids certainly do love the attention. Who wouldn't? It's only natural. But with proper guidance from the parents, most children easily place this business in its proper perspective. It requires hard work, discipline, and persistence for the kids, and they are proud of their accomplishments. For every headline about a child supposedly gone bad from being in show business and for every story of a spoiled stage brat, there are thousands of children having a great time, learning new skills, and gaining confidence.

For the vast majority of the children, auditioning and working is a part-time activity, not something that overwhelms their lives. Of course there are periods when audition calls come in several times a week. It will get a little hectic trying to arrange schedules and fight the traffic, but then the phone may not ring for weeks at a time. Veteran parents usually proceed with the attitude of "going for it while it's happening." You're never quite sure what will be going on in the near future. The needs of the industry change. Certain "types" and age brackets may be in hot demand for a while and then suddenly go cold. Accurately predicting how busy your child will be is almost impossible. It will depend on many things: age, looks, talent, representation, timing, and photos—just to name a few.

A child working *regularly,* as in a weekly television series, is a different matter altogether. Depending on the circumstances, that child and his parents will more than likely experience quite a change in their lives. But these children are a rare few, and the situation does not come about by accident.

Landing a role on a series is something that is desired and worked toward by the parents and child. It is not for everyone.

The average child, however, may work only five or six times a year shooting a few commercials and maybe a couple of small parts on a television show or in a motion picture. Most children will generally stay in the business for a few years and then move on to other things. It is a small percentage who remain in the business into their late teens and beyond. At that time, they are usually more interested in other activities and are thinking of college and other careers.

As with most activities or businesses, there will be expenses—photos, union dues, maybe some classes, that type of thing. But these are expenses that should come *later*. Your initial money outlay will be minimal. There will be more on this in following chapters.

You may also be worried about the "rejection" part of this business, and how your child—and you for that matter—will handle it. Once again, it all comes down to attitude. If you, the parent/manager, become too serious or create a pressure atmosphere of tension or jealousy, then, yes, there is a good chance that rejection—and even working itself—will have a negative effect on your child. If, on the other hand, you view it all as a positive and learning experience, your child will do fine.

Rejection is a part of life. How it is handled is the key. Not making the starting lineup on the Little League team or failing to win the starring role in the Christmas play at school are also forms of rejection. But feeling hurt or disappointed is no reason to quit, or not give the activity a chance. Try your best, Give it a shot, Make the attempt—those sayings are all communicating the same message. Allowing the *fear* of failure to stop someone from even trying could have far worse consequences than any temporary "rejection."

More than likely, a child who is talented enough to get started in this business has enough on the ball to not take the auditions too personally. This is especially true when combined with good support and patient explanations from the parent. For example: A child does a wonderful job on an audition. The casting director may even take you aside afterward and tell you how terrific he was (something rarely done, by the way). He is called back twice more to meet other people. And for all that, he *still* doesn't land the part. Maybe he was an inch too tall, or his hair was the wrong color, or perhaps he didn't match the other actors well enough to create a "real family" look, or maybe the child who eventually got the part said his lines in a quirky little way that gave him the edge. Those things are out of your child's control. It does not mean they didn't like him or that he failed or anything like that. Frustrating? Yes, very much so at times. But frustration is not the same as rejection. It is important to understand that not getting picked for every audition is a very real part of being in this business. Just like real life.

Commercial auditions, especially, should not be taken too seriously. You may find it amazing that more than a hundred children may be auditioned just to find one to shout the word "YUMMY!," but that's the way it's done. All other things considered, the auditioning part of this business has a lot to do with numbers: The more your child does, the better his chances of working. If you, the parent/manager, are going to take each lost job personally, then you should think twice about getting started—for your sake and for that of the child. Children are very perceptive, especially the bright, talented kids in this business. They are usually quite aware of any anxieties and pressures clouding over their parents. This can affect their performance on the auditions and possibly in their everyday lives.

That is why this book was written for the family who sees working in the entertainment business as something fun to do, an enjoyable experience the entire family can share. With the right attitude and guidance, a child may enjoy many profitable years of working and still lead a very normal, happy kid's life.

3

I Know My Kid Is Cute, But Is That Enough?

So, where do you begin? How do you actually get this idea into motion? The answer is, by first asking yourself another tough question: "How do I know if my child really has what it takes?" Don't try to fool yourself with the answer. There is a lot of opportunity out there, more so than ever before. But there is also more competition. And the competition is good. A child must have a composite of qualities. It is not as simple as being cute or having an extra-nice smile. Those are good qualities to have but are not enough. It is not a matter of one or two special ingredients. This is difficult for some parents to understand, especially if their daughter has just won first prize in the last six beauty pageants she has entered. What is really desired are creative, happy, outgoing kids who are able to listen, follow directions, have a good attention span, get along well with adults and other children, and can think on their feet. *That's* the basic material to begin with.

Read and answer the following questions very carefully. You should be able to determine for yourself if your child qualifies at this time.

Personality

1. Is your child outgoing and spontaneous in his communication with adults—not just giving yes or no answers, but willing to communicate more than is asked? Will he originate and freely join in conversations?
2. Is there a real spark in the eyes? Does he show the spirit and enthusiasm of just being a kid?
3. Does your child maintain good eye contact while speaking or listening?
4. Can your child stay focused on one subject or project for an extended period of time? Auditioning and working will require this ability.
5. Does your child have a high energy level? One that is controllable?

Quite often, a child may demonstrate some or all of these qualities at home, but will get shy and quiet when around strangers. If that is the case, the child is not ready. Agents and personal managers who work with children are very used to hearing the following words from a parent whose child was just turned down for representation: "I don't understand it, he's always putting on shows and entertaining our friends and relatives. And I bet he knows the words to fifty commercials." All well and good, but he must be willing to demonstrate that talent and enthusiasm in public, in front of strangers. Those qualities should come naturally, without a lot of prodding or begging.

Desire

One of the first things an agent or personal manager will look for is the child's willingness to be in commercials. In other words, is this something the child is genuinely interested in, or is it an idea that mom and dad cooked up on their own? It is not unusual for a youngster to suddenly find himself standing in an agent's office, in the middle of an interview, without the slightest idea as to why he is there. This doesn't necessarily mean the parents have bad intentions or that they are forcing the child into this business. It often just never dawns on them to ask the simple question: "Would you like to be on TV like those other kids?"

This is a major consideration in starting your child. It is a mistake to assume that your child cannot make a decision like this. Sometimes children do not know if they want to participate in a certain activity because they do not have a clear understanding of what is involved. While you are watching commercials (especially those using children), try asking your child if this is something he would like to do. If you have access to a camcorder, set up a pretend audition or a pretend commercial for your child and let him observe the results. Ask him what he thinks about it. Was it fun? Was it something he would like to do again? Explain to him what it *really* means.

If your child is very young, and asking such a question is not yet possible, then your evaluation will have to be based on your knowledge and observation of the child around other adults and children.

You should be realistic about your child and about the things he will be expected to do. Preparation can be a big help. Most kids do a very good job at playing Let's Pretend, and that's really what this business is all about.

Discipline

1. Is your child willing to be given directions by other adults?
2. Will he understand and follow directions easily without making a lot of comments in return?
3. Is your child overly influenced by other children's actions?

It is not stated in a rule book anywhere, but the three areas just covered—*personality, desire,* and *discipline*—are probably the most important to consider.

Now, let's take a look at a few more important qualities.

Speech

1. Some children have quirky or unusual voices that are interesting and acceptable in certain situations; and of course, some commercials do not have speaking roles. But generally, the voice should be clear and easy to understand.
2. If your child slurs his words, speaks too slowly or rapidly, or has a heavy accent, then his difficulty would have to be overcome first.

Physical Characteristics

From your own experience, you've probably come to realize that all types of children are used in commercials, TV series, and motion pictures. This is one reason why there is a continuing demand for children. A talent representative (agent or manager) will want to have a variety of children to fit the various age brackets and "looks" that are requested.

For example, one category in an agent's office might read:

"Six-to-eight-year-old boys." Filling out that category would be six-to-eight-year-old African American boys, six-to-eight-year-old Asian boys, six-to-eight-year-old Hispanic boys, six-to-eight-year-old boys with red hair and freckles, and so forth.

But no matter what the "look," there are other important factors relating to physical appearance.

Height

It is preferable that a child be average or below average in height for his age. If a child is tall for his age, it may make him appear older and he would have to compete in that older age bracket—a difficult task to ask of a young kid. Agents would rather have a seven- or eight-year-old who looks six, not the other way around.

Body Size

There is no hard and fast rule here. As with the adult actors, child actors come in all shapes and sizes. Generally speaking, average physical dimensions are required most of the time. Young girls who are overly developed for their age and boys who are overly muscular and "bulked out" will appear to be older.

Teeth

1. Not necessarily perfect, but the teeth should be straight and good-looking. If any of the front teeth are missing, the child may have to wear a "flipper." Flippers are artificial teeth worn *only* on auditions or when *working*. They are so named because they are easily "flipped" in and out of the mouth.

2. Crooked, overlapping, chipped, or stained teeth will have to be taken care of. Most advertisers—especially for food products—insist on good-looking teeth.

3. In most cases, if your child wears braces, he will have to wait until they are removed. You will occasionally see a child with braces on TV, but it is the exception rather than the rule.

Age

Personal choice and ability will often determine the right age to start. The majority of work for children occurs after the age of four or five. The age of six, however, is when things can really take off. The reason is that after six, a child can legally put in a full day's work on the set—very often an important consideration. If the final casting choice on a job is between a five-year-old and a legal six-year-old, the odds are in favor of the six-year-old getting the nod. If your child is four or five and has the right qualities, then that could be a great time to get started. By the time he reaches six and enters the busier age bracket, he will have a year or two of experience behind him.

Agents and managers tend to be very particular when taking on a child twelve or older because the child will often be competing with children who have already been in the business for several years. Of course, this does not mean that the older kids don't have a chance. They certainly do. They just really have to be on the ball, meet all the qualifying criteria, and show real potential and strong desire. Some professional training such as a good commercial workshop will also help. School plays and community theater also provide great experience and will show that the older child is serious about pursuing work in the industry.

But no matter what the age—nine, fourteen, six, or

eleven—a child's looking younger than his actual age is a definite asset. It will improve his chances of getting representation and landing jobs.

Now let's use a quick checklist for review. How many can you mark as a Yes in evaluating your child for this business? Be honest. Your child is the way he is. If he does not fit the criteria for getting involved, then that's okay.

Personality _____   Desire _____
Discipline _____   Speech _____
Physical Characteristics:
Height _____   Teeth _____
Body Size _____

Now let's say that you were able to answer Yes to all of the above, but you're still not absolutely sure; or maybe some of your Yes answers are borderline . . . what then? An excellent way to determine your final answer would be to enroll your child in a professional commercial workshop. For a period of six to eight weeks, the children are exposed to what it's really like to go on a commercial audition. They are shown how to work in front of a video camera, the various techniques for properly demonstrating actions, and how to say lines. At the end of the class, your decision should be evident. Even children who are "naturals" for working in commercials will often find that a workshop is very rewarding. They learn in a class what they would otherwise have to learn on the actual auditions. Training is not absolutely necessary, but should be considered. Confidence is very important, and learning and practicing proper audition techniques helps build it.

You should also keep in mind that some of these things will change. Teeth come and go. Growth spurts can occur. A desire to "be on TV and make lots of commercials" may suddenly become the most important thing in little Johnny's life (at least for a while), and shy Jennifer may change practically overnight into a confident, talkative, outgoing personality.

Evaluate now . . . reevaluate later.

4

WHAT ABOUT BABIES?

There's no doubt plenty of work out there for the baby set—especially in commercials. Turn on your TV any time of the day or night and it won't be long before one of these little cuties crawls, giggles, or toddles across the screen. One little gurgle or smile and your heart is stolen. And you can bet the advertising people are aware of that fact. That's why the little ones are not limited only to commercials touting baby products. You name it: tires, phone companies, hamburgers, floor wax—almost any product you've seen advertised on TV has at one time probably used a baby in its commercials.

Contrary to one popular belief, the babies you see on TV are *not* related to the director or producer—or a close personal friend. In almost all cases, those working babies have agents and/or managers and go on audition calls just like the older children. Nepotism may occur now and then, but very rarely.

Another confusing and widely held belief is the one concerning twins: "They only use twins when working with babies in commercials and movies." That idea is far from accurate. It is true that, in an ideal situation, a production company would probably prefer to hire a set of twins over a single baby. There are two reasons for this:

1. Due to the strict time limitations under which a baby may work, having an identical twin around could theoretically double the on-camera time available.
2. There is always the possibility that one baby may be in a cranky mood or just does not want to cooperate. If that happens, they can bring in baby number 2 and no one is the wiser. (When not using twins, one or two back-up babies are usually hired and available on the set, just in case.)

The problem with this ideal situation is obvious: there just are not that many twins around. And even if a set of twins is auditioning for a part, it still comes down to the bottom line of what the people doing the hiring may be looking for: personality, type, or enough resemblance to the adult actors to create a "real family" look. The twins might have an advantage going in and may even get a second look because of that, but if they're not right for the spot—they're not right.

Not all children's agencies represent babies, but those that do have something they usually refer to as their "Baby Files." Babies can work legally any time after fifteen days of age in California, so an agent's files will probably have little ones listed ranging from newborn on up. These files, of course, require a constant influx of new faces if they are to remain current. It does not take long for a baby to move out of one category—such as six to nine months—and into another. As with older children, casting calls will usually come in asking for an age bracket and type: newborn, four to six months, eight to twelve months, etc. The variations of age brackets requested can be very narrow (babies no older than two months) or quite wide (babies from six to eighteen months). Ideally, an agency would like to have the right babies to send on each audition.

Agents have different procedures regarding babies and how they work with them. Some are not interested in meeting each baby in person but will base their decision of representation on photos they have seen and information provided to them by the parents. Others make it a practice to have a "baby day" and bring all the possible candidates in for a personal look. Another agency may, after first seeing a photo, bring in each baby individually. Some agencies rely on personal managers to provide the right baby for an audition.

The requirements for babies are not that dissimilar from the older children. Babies should demonstrate most of the following characteristics:

1. Happy and alert
2. Outgoing
3. Curious and interested in other people
4. Comfortable in new surroundings
5. Allow themselves to be held by strangers
6. Should look their age

There *are* many opportunities for the little ones, but in comparison to older children, the number of auditions you will attend in a year's time will probably be very small. Keep in mind that each audition requires different babies in accordance with their age and type. Rarely does a call go out asking for something like: "Babies, all kinds, all ages up to two-and-a-half needed." The requirements that are usually requested limit the number of auditions your baby will go on.

This will change as your child grows older and into the more popular age brackets. So don't get discouraged. You're just getting started and have many years ahead of you.

Because babies go through so many changes in such a short period of time, it is essential that the agent always has current photos and information about your baby. If an agent goes through his or her files and pulls out a picture of a six-month-old who is now twelve months old, that file may very well end up in the trash. The agent may or may not be willing to take the time to call parents asking for new photos. *That is and should be your responsibility.* By updating photos and information, you are also showing that you are reliable and really interested in pursuing work for your child. A problem that often occurs with a baby's parents is their failure to do the things necessary to actually advance their baby's chances for working on commercials or motion pictures. That's understandable. New parents are usually so caught up in the joy (and hard work) of caring for their little one that it's easy to forget about such things as updating photos for the agent. But it's important to stay with it. Approach your child's involvement in the entertainment business with a professional attitude. Check with the agency that accepts your baby as to the period of time preferred between updates, but a good rule of thumb is about three to four months.

5

AGENTS

Often on the receiving end of many Hollywood jokes, agents are vital in the framework of this business. Agents are the people who set up auditions for their clients and negotiate contracts. That's the basics. They are often involved in a hundred and one other important activities. It *is* possible to get a job for your child on your own—by contacting an advertising agency directly or maybe through a friend of a friend sort of thing—but without legitimate representation from a qualified agent, your child's chances of landing major commercials or working on a TV series or motion picture are practically zero.

In exchange for their work, agents receive a 10% commission on the gross amount of money your child will earn. For example, your child receives a check for a commercial he has worked on. The gross amount of the check is $828. The agent will receive 10% of that amount, or $82.80. Your child will receive the remainder, minus taxes.

You should seek out talent agencies that are franchised by the unions: the Screen Actors Guild (SAG) and the American Federation of Television and Radio Artists (AFTRA). You will pay nothing in advance to these agencies. Agents associated with the unions do not earn money by selling anything (e.g., photos, classes, or information) to their clients. Their incomes are dependent upon their clients' success. In California, talent agencies are licensed by the state as Artists Talent Agents.

What Is a Good Agency?

Ask ten people to define a good agency and you may get ten different replies. It depends on what a person needs or looks for in an agency. Generally speaking, a good agency will be well established with good contacts, have experienced and knowledgeable personnel, and will be able to provide a great number of auditions for its client list.

Like any other business, you will find all types of talent agencies. They range from the "mom and pop" type to the corporate. The size can vary wildly. One may employ only a couple of people and represent a small, select number of clients. Another may be very large and represent hundreds of clients. Some may specialize in children, others in adults, and still others in the full spectrum of infants to seniors. The quality of the agency is not determined by its size or how expensive the front door looks, but rather by the job the agents are doing for their clients. Getting the right agent for your child is very important, but don't get caught up in an image of what you *think* an agency should look like. You shouldn't be put off if the first agent you visit is working out of a cramped office, filled with photos and ringing telephones. It may be a terrific agency for your child. The agency around the corner with the plush carpeting, exotic plants, and designer waiting room may also be fine—or maybe not. The point is: Don't rely on image alone.

It *is* okay to change agents. If you find that things are not working out, it is probably a good idea to seek new representation for your child. *A word of warning:* Do not get in the habit of "agent hopping" every few weeks or months. You must give your agent an opportunity to work with your child. This is especially true if you are new to the business. Most agencies are always looking for quality talent, but more than likely they will already have many talented kids who have been with the agency awhile and are experienced and working. Your child cannot expect the same degree of attention as the veteran kids who are currently bringing in the money to pay the rent. It takes time to work into this business.

There is also something to be said for loyalty, sometimes a touchy subject with agents and managers. It is often the case that an agent or manager may devote a lot of attention to someone for a couple of years and then, just as the client starts doing really well, gets left in the dust for another company. The agent or manager who is willing to start from scratch with you and your child deserves fair treatment. If your agency has been working hard for your child, then stay with it. It is not the agent's fault if your child has been doing a lot of auditions but not landing the jobs. However, let's say that the number of auditions has dropped dramatically over the last couple of months. That's reason to take notice, but not an automatic condemnation of your agent. Maybe things are just generally slow all around; maybe there has been very little going on for your child's type and age; maybe the agent is sending your child's picture all over town for possible auditions, but no one is interested in seeing him. Those are all legitimate reasons for a slowdown. You can't do much about the first two except wait for busier times. And if the pictures continue to elicit no response, maybe it's time for a new look. The correct thing to do when experiencing a noticeable lack of auditions for a period of time is to talk to your agent. Ask how things are going. Don't be afraid to ask if he or she is still enthusiastic about your child.

An agency is risking time, energy, and some expense with each client it represents. You are doing the same with each agency you become involved with. It's a two-way street. Expenses such as professional pictures and classes can add up.

The number of agents you can find to represent your child will vary depending upon location. Check with your local Screen Actors Guild for what is appropriate in your area. In Los Angeles, the rule is one for each market: one agent for commercials and one for theatrical (movies and TV). Or, you can have one agent to represent you in both markets. An ideal situation is to find an agency that is good in all areas. *But* if you are new, your primary interest should be in commercial representation. That's the right place to start. If you are also seeking print work for your child (magazines, posters, etc.), you might want more than one agent for that purpose. Some agents allow multiple representation for print work. Ask first, and be careful if you choose that route. It's easy to get your wires crossed.

Some agents will have you sign a contract when they accept your child as a client. Others may have you sign a contract after your child has landed his first job. Signing a contract does not mean the agent will work harder for you, nor will it make your child do a better job on the auditions. Among other things, one of the primary points of the contract is to ensure that the agency has a written agreement with the client when it comes time to collect commissions. Take your time and read the contract over. Get all questions answered to your satisfaction. Keep in mind that agents will not take your child on as a client unless they see real potential. Agents are in business to make money. A contract will not influence their feelings about your child.

It should be noted that agents *represent* their clients to casting people, producers, directors, etc. The same may be said in reverse. Each time parents or young actors are out there meeting the people who influence or make decisions, they are *representing* their agents. Behaving in an unprofessional manner will more than likely get back to the agent. Act accordingly. Conduct yourself as you would expect your agent to.

6

GETTING THE AGENT

word of caution here. Parents are most vulnerable during the hopeful search for someone who agrees that their son or daughter is indeed the next Rising Star. All parents love to hear how "wonderfully talented and bright and absolutely perfect" their children are. It's only natural. But there are people who will take advantage of this pride and enthusiasm and attempt to maneuver unsuspecting parents into buying everything from expensive photo sessions to classes and even a new wardrobe. Professional photos *are* needed, but not necessarily *before* getting an agent. Classes *may* be needed, but not as a stipulation of representation (e.g., "Your child has potential, but I will only take him on if he enrolls in one of the commercial classes I teach."). Get another opinion. A new wardrobe? Not really necessary.

So, how do you go about finding one of these good agents for your future star? There are a few ways to begin, but if at all possible, get several recommendations from someone who is already in the business. That person could be a friend or neighbor, or someone you meet at a beauty pageant or school play or Little League game. Once you begin asking around, you'll probably be surprised by how many people have their children in commercials (or did at one time). If they are willing to help, they might be able to lead you to the right agent. You may also be surprised to find them reluctant to give out valuable information like that. In their minds, they're looking at possible competition for their own children!

If you cannot get a recommendation, then your next step is to refer to the Talent Unions listed at the end of this book. As stated earlier, these organizations will be able to provide you with a copy of the current agency list for your area. This list will contain all of the franchised agents and should be coded in such a way as to determine which of them have children's departments. As a last option, check the Yellow Pages of your local phone book under the heading Talent Agents.

You may want to call the agencies first and ask if they are looking for new children to add to their client roster and, if so, what ages and types they're most interested in. That may save you some time and postage. If they're not in need of someone like your child, that's good information to have. It's usually not a good idea to be with an agency that represents many children similar in age and type to yours.

Taking Photographs

After selecting the agents, your next step will be to send pictures and some information regarding your child. It's important to keep in mind that at this stage, *you are only trying to get the agents interested*. Spending a lot of money on professional pictures, prior to getting an agent, is usually out of sequence. Most agents will accept a good series of amateur pictures of your child. These can be taken by you, a friend, or a relative. If an agent is interested, he will want to see the child in person. This is especially true of younger children. As kids begin to move into their early teens, it may become more difficult to generate interest with just a few snapshots, but try to stick with that method.

You could be doing yourself a big favor by waiting to do professional pictures. There is the very real possibility that even though your child seems to have all the right qualities for working in commercials, he just cannot get an agent interested enough to take him on as a client. Also, by waiting, your agent can tell you exactly what is needed in the way of hairstyles, what type of clothing your child should wear, and whether to use any props. Agents are understandably fussy when it comes to their clients' pictures. Some like to represent their clients with a simple head shot. Others prefer to use a composite of several pictures in a variety of poses. If asked, agents can recommend several professionals who know exactly what needs to be done. Your local studio photographer down at the mall may be very good at what he or she does, but probably does not have a lot of experience in shooting photo sessions specifically for this business. There is a big difference between a theatrical or commercial head shot and a studio portrait to hang over your fireplace. Nine times out of ten, when using a photographer not experienced in shooting pictures for the entertainment industry, the end result will not be right. There is a very specific look and attitude that should be evident in a theatrical or commercial picture.

Note: Agents (or anyone, for that matter) should never *insist* that you use the one photographer they recommended. They may have preferences and like the work a particular photographer does, but the final choice is yours. This is mentioned only because of the confusing and often misleading information about pictures. Shop for a photographer as you would any other professional. Ask agents, managers, and others already in the business for recommendations. Ask to see examples of the photographer's work. Get at least two or three price quotes.

The pictures you send in to an agency should not be just any old thing left over from last summer's vacation. Little Andrew might look real cute standing next to Goofy in the middle of Disney World, but it's not what we need here. On any given week, a good kids' agency, especially one that is well established, will receive a very large number of photos in the mail. Every single one of those are of children seeking representation, just like yours. The competition begins at this point. The photos you send are going to have to "sell" your child. Start thinking show biz. Imagine the picture you're sending lying in a stack several inches deep. Is there something special about it? Does it really capture your child's personality? Is there anything distracting about it? Maybe you're too biased. Ask a friend or neighbor for an honest opinion. And keep this one thought: *Real kids . . . they're looking for real kids!* Not little businessmen in suits and ties; not glamorous six-year-old starlets in fashionable exercise clothing. Choose appropriate clothing to enhance your child, not distract from him.

Here are a few guidelines to follow when taking your own pictures:

1. Standard 35-mm camera preferred. Use color film to enhance your child's characteristics and to create a nice, lively look. (Black-and-white photography is done by the professional.)
2. Your child's face or body should be the prominent part of the picture—at least 65% to 75%. It's difficult

to get a sense of someone's personality and looks if the photo was taken from fifteen feet away.

3. Avoid profiles.
4. Give the pictures a candid look, relaxed instead of formal.
5. Fad clothing, bizarre hairstyles, heavy makeup, and jewelry look out of place. Remember, "real kids" doing "real things."
6. Only one child in the picture. Group shots are distracting and will only confuse the viewer.
7. Shoot two or more rolls of film. The more shots, the better your chances of getting a few good ones.
8. Busy backgrounds can draw attention away from the main subject. Keep them simple.
9. Shoot in natural light, outdoors. This gives the photos an easy, relaxed look.
10. Watch for shadows and squinting of the eyes.

The photos should have a candid look to them, but can be planned in advance. For instance, think of three or four scenes, write them in a notebook, and title each one, e.g., "Andrew Plays Baseball." Then plan your wardrobe and props around each scene. In this case, under the wardrobe heading, you could write: T-shirt, jeans, cap, and sneakers. For props, how about: baseball, glove, bat, and bench. Now you're ready to do your photo session with no interruptions. Shoot head shots (approximately mid-chest and up) and body shots in each scene.

This may sound like a lot of extra effort. "Why not just take a couple of pictures in the front yard, send one in, and see what happens?" you might be saying to yourself. Well, there is a chance that will work well enough to grab an agent's attention. But there are advantages to the methods described above:

1. This is good practice for working in front of a camera. Your child will have to listen and follow directions.

2. Up to this point, the idea of being in commercials and movies may be a bit vague to your child. Talking about why you are taking photos and planning a photo session together will help make the prospect of working more concrete.

3. First impressions! Your child is also now your client. Present him in the best way you can. Your goal should be to have the agent looking forward to meeting your child.

4. This will be the first opportunity for you and your child to actually work together on a project specifically for the entertainment business—something you may be doing frequently in the future.

(Note: Please see the Wardrobe chapter of this book for tips on clothing and colors.)

Suggestions for Babies

Most of the steps that apply to older children will also apply to babies, including:

1. Show what baby can do: sit, crawl, stand, etc.

2. Keep clothing simple. Avoid turtlenecks and a bulky look.

3. Shoot the pictures on their level, not looking down on them.

4. Don't take pictures with baby flat on back.

5. Don't show arm support if possible.

6. No "messy food" pictures. Bowls of cereal turned upside down on baby's head might be cute to you, but won't work here.

7. No "baby starlet" pictures, e.g., sunglasses, makeup, earrings, etc.

Getting good photos of a baby is often on a par with taking pictures of a frisky puppy. It is almost always a two-person job—one to work the camera, another to attract the baby's attention so that you can capture those big, generous smiles and quirky expressions. If it doesn't work one day, try again the next. And, of course, make sure your little one is well fed and rested prior to the photo session.

"So what happens if I'm a real klutz with a camera?" you might ask. Well, don't be afraid to ask friends and relatives. Remember those great pictures Uncle Bob took last Thanksgiving? He'd probably love to give you a hand with this. Who knows, your child may respond differently and do a better job in front of a nonparent anyway. If all else does fail, though (it does happen—some people just can't take a good picture), then your only choice is to hire a professional.

Whether you hire the professional before getting an agent or afterward, the procedure is the same. First, you want to be sure the photographer has lots of experience in working with children. Some photographers specialize in the younger set, or tend to do a lot of work with kids. They will probably do a better job of capturing a relaxed, natural look than the photographer who only occasionally does a kid's shoot. As noted earlier, you should also ask to see several examples of the photographer's work. Then determine if the general format is in line with what you are looking for.

The photographer should take two to four rolls of film showing your child in a variety of poses, expressions, and wardrobe. A few days after the session, the photographer will have developed proof sheets, also called contact sheets, which are sheets showing small prints (about $1\frac{1}{2} \times 1$ inches each) of all the pictures on one roll of developed film. These are studied closely with a magnifying glass or photographer's magnifying loop. Several of the smaller prints are chosen and then blown up to an 8 × 10-inch "master" print size. From these blow-ups, the decision is made as to which picture (or pictures) will be used to represent your child. Picture selection is usually done by your agent and in concurrence with your manager if you have one. Do not be surprised if their selection differs from what you might have chosen. They are looking at the photos strictly from a business viewpoint; in other words, what will work best in attracting the right kind of attention for your child. A parent is usually not objective enough to make this important decision. You will have to trust their knowledge and experience.

Finally, the master prints are sent to a company that specializes in photo printing and will reproduce several hundred copies. Your child's name and other information such as date of birth, hair and eye color, agency logo, manager's name, etc., are added to the photo. Your agent will keep at least half of the pictures for purposes of submitting them to casting directors.

Please note that the professional photos are always done in black and white. Do not use color. Because so many copies of a single head shot may be needed, color pictures are cost-prohibitive.

As you can see, there is a lot involved in getting professional pictures made up—not to mention that by the time you have hired the photographer and printed two or three hundred copies (normal amount), you have invested a few hundred dollars. So, to repeat once again: Try the home-done version first. Try to get an agent interested and your child into the business. Then let your agent assist you in getting exactly what he or she will need to represent your child. It is not unusual for a naive parent to invest several hundred dollars in a photo session, only to hear from the new agent: "Okay, we'd like to represent your child, but the first thing we'll need are some new, *good* pictures."

Sending the Pictures

Because most agencies receive a large number of pictures each week, it's a good idea to present yours in a professional manner. This makes a good impression, and the agents will appreciate your consideration of their time. A couple of Polaroids wrapped in a messy, handwritten note will not win a lot of points. To begin with, on the back of *every picture* you should print your child's name, date of birth, and home phone number. It's easy for a single snapshot—or a half dozen for that matter—to get mislaid within the busy confines of an agent's office. And it's not unusual to hear "Does anyone know this kid?" shouted across a bustling office in the hope that someone has a name and phone number to match a picture.

Submitting your pictures in a clear plastic sleeve makes good sense, especially if sending two or more poses. Choose a sleeve with pockets or slots to hold three or four pictures. In this way, the pictures you are sending can be displayed in a manner similar to a professional composite. Composites are approximately 8½ × 11 inches and show the actor in a variety of wardrobes, hairstyles, and expressions. If you are sending more than one pose, limit your number to no more than four. That is more than sufficient. The plastic also allows for handling without fear of damage. Include a *brief* letter with the pictures, introducing your child and stating that you're looking for representation (see sample).

Although you may be tempted to do otherwise, keep the letter short and sweet. Don't overdo it. The agent is going to be most interested in the pictures and *specific* information. Gushing on and on with parental pride about how "everyone

Date

Agent's Name
Street Address
City, State Zip

Dear (Agent),

I am currently seeking representation for my son Kellen. He is seven years old, has sandy blond hair and brown eyes.

Kellen is all boy, excelling in sports and bubbling with energy. He is outgoing, spontaneous, follows directions well, and gets along with other children and adults.

I have enclosed two photos. If you are interested in Kellen, we would be happy to meet with you at your convenience.

Sincerely,

Parent's Name
(Telephone Number)

says he should be in commercials" is not something an agent has time for.

Include with the pictures and letter a typed information sheet. This is similar to a résumé (see sample). This sheet should include labeled spaces for name, height, weight, date of birth, hair and eye color, training or experience, special skills, and sports. Don't overlook any of the things your child can do. You will want to include all of this information—no matter how unimportant it may seem to you. The more skills and talents a child has, the greater his chances of at least being noticed. For example, let's say that nine-year-old Eric is just average in his communication skills, but really excels in several sports and activities such as roller blading, tricks on his BMX, gymnastics, and ice-skating. Eric may get the nod for representation based on his multiple skills with the understanding that he'll need to work on his communication and audition techniques. He would be chosen for representation because of the great number of commercials utilizing children in various hobbies or pastimes. If a commercial spot calls for kids who are "experienced on a pogo stick and stilts" (it does happen), then an agent will go through his or her files in the hopes of finding someone for that audition.

Okay, next step. Clip all of this together, pictures, letter, and information sheet, and send to the agents you have selected. Address to Children's Department. Keep accurate records of what you sent, when, and where. Should you follow up with a phone call? Good question. There is no hard and fast rule here. Some agencies do not mind a quick, courteous call inquiring about pictures sent. Others quite adamantly maintain a "Don't call us, we'll call you if we're interested" policy. In most cases, if the photos are good and if the agency does have a need for children like yours, you *will* receive a call. The fact is that talent agencies do need a continuing supply of new

Child's Name Here
(social security number)

Date of Birth: Height:

Age: Weight:

Hair:

Eyes:

Training/Classes (list name of class and instructor)

Commercial Workshop

Drama

Dance (include what kind, duration, and instructor)*

Special Skills

Swimming, Frisbee, Ice- and Roller-skating, Skateboarding, Snow Skiing, Basketball, Gymnastics (three years),* Horseback Riding

Address and Phone Number

*List length of time and level of proficiency only for skills that your child excels in, *or* for skills not considered everyday normal activities. It is understood by agents and managers that all other skills are performed at an average level.

faces. Children grow up and change, they drop out of the business, they move to another state, a change in scheduling suddenly no longer allows a parent the time to run to auditions. Those are the facts. Be patient. If your child has many of the qualities discussed earlier, someone *will* be interested. Don't be surprised to hear from an agency several weeks after you sent your material. The agents may just be getting around to looking at your pictures.

When you do talk to an agent, be honest with your answers to any questions he or she may have. In other words, don't exaggerate your child's abilities or experience. Falsely telling an agent that your child is an expert singer with six years of training and has starred in the last five productions at your local community theater will only backfire at a later date.

Agents will be honest in their reactions to your child's pictures and information. They have nothing to gain by being otherwise. If they are not interested, it does not mean they didn't like your child or think that he's not right for this business. They may already have a child similar to yours in looks and age range, or they simply may not be accepting new children at the time. Or, they . . . just . . . are . . . not . . . interested. Simple as that. Nothing personal. Don't give up, and *don't get discouraged. Go on to the next agent on your list!* If ever there was a business where one could receive a variety of opinions, show business is it.

Agents have different policies about interviewing children. The age of the child is often a factor. Some agents don't care to work with kids under three or four years of age. If this is the case, but they still like your child's pictures, they may say they will put the photos in their files and call if any auditions come up. Thank them and continue contacting other agents. Try to get an interview. There is nothing like an agent meeting your child in person.

The Agent Interview

When an agent does set up an interview for your child, it means he or she is interested—that's all! It is not a guarantee of acceptance. The impression your child makes on the agent at that meeting is very important. Prepare your child by letting him know why he is going and what to expect. Most agent interviews are similar to an actual commercial audition. They will usually begin by asking simple questions of the child and then have him demonstrate the commercial dialogue learned in the waiting room.

To repeat: Agents are looking for children who can speak easily with adults and are willing to answer questions with more than just a yes or no. If the question is "Do you have any pets at home?" and the child does, then a good reply would sound something like, "Yes, we've got a big gray cat and two goldfish. Smoky is the cat's name and he's always trying to eat the fish, but I won't let him." Obviously, you cannot—nor should you even try to—put words in a child's mouth. But you get the idea. Have your child work on fully answering simple questions like:

> "Where do you go to school?"
> "What's your favorite food?"
> "What kind of games do you like to play?"
> "Do you have any pets?"
> "What's your favorite cartoon?"

Also ask questions requiring your child to think on his feet:

> "Why do you want to be on TV?"
> "If I gave you a hundred dollars and said you had to spend it, what would you buy?"
> "What if you were eating a foot-long hot dog, and a big

glob of mustard suddenly squirted onto your shirt. What kind of face would you make and what would you say?"

Preparation at home beforehand is the key to a successful interview. A few question-and-answer practice sessions could really help. Encourage your child to give answers that offer more information and can lead to a little conversation. Try creating a make-believe commercial and have your child repeat it several times without it growing stale. Practice basic emotions: happy, sad, mad. But be careful not to overdo it and *never, never* show how you would do it. Encourage the child to do it in his own way.

Of course, your child cannot be forced into demonstrating an ability he does not have. Allow him to do the best he can and let it go at that.

Practicing Basic Emotions

(Angry) Mom, I'm hungry. What's for dinner?
(Sad) Mom, I'm hungry. What's for dinner?
(Happy) Mom, I'm hungry. What's for dinner?

Include "pretending" in your practice sessions. During auditions, the child should realistically appear to be doing whatever is called for.

Examples

"Pretend that you're opening a jar of peanut butter and making a sandwich."
"Pretend that you're holding a doll in your arms. Rock it back and forth, then bend down and kiss it good night."
"Pretend that it's late at night and you're sneaking into the

kitchen for a snack. Just as you open the refrigerator, someone turns on the light and catches you. Make a surprised face."

The key point of pretending is to really look as if you're doing whatever you are pretending to do. Quick hand motions or halfhearted attempts are not enough. If the child is asked to pretend to eat a hamburger, he should go through all of the usual physical actions: pick it up, bring it to his mouth, take a bite, chew for a moment, then swallow.

Those are the kinds of things agents are looking for. Why? Because that's what is needed on commercial auditions. But these are just suggestions. Don't get too carried away, or you'll run the risk of overcoaching or making your child feel anxious. Remember, you're just learning too. Another thing to consider is enrollment in a commercial workshop. A good workshop will properly prepare a beginning actor for auditions. The actor will learn where to stand, the correct use of hand motions, how to achieve eye contact with the camera, how to work effectively with other actors, and the correct way to say commercial copy.

It's okay for your child to be a little nervous at the interview. An agent's job is to spot potential, and he or she will probably take into consideration a small case of butterflies. But excessive movement, hands in the mouth, low volume, and looking at the floor or ceiling won't go over well. Be careful to avoid putting too much pressure on your child. Have fun in your practice sessions at home. Getting started in commercials should be an activity your child enjoys. After all, he's the one who'll be going in to that agent's office or standing in front of a video camera for an audition, not you.

If an audition prospect seems like too much for your child to confront at this time, then that's all there is to it. Wait a few months and see how the child responds then. No one wins if you try to push them. Some children are naturals for working in commercials and movies; others do well after a little time and effort. If your child really shows a strong desire to get involved in the entertainment business, then encourage and work with him.

Just as all commercial and theatrical auditions are slightly different from one another, agent interviews will also vary. Some may last only a few minutes; others will be much longer. One agent may ask the child to memorize a commercial script, then recite it. Another may be more interested in your child's ability to just stand there and hold a conversation. The degree of difficulty of the interview will, of course, be determined by the age of the child. A ten- or twelve-year-old will be expected to do much more than a child of five or six.

(Note: For more tips on interview preparation, please refer to the Auditions chapter.)

After the interview is complete, the agent will respond in one of the following ways: "Yes, we're interested in representing your child," or "No thank you," or suggest your child attend a professional commercial workshop and return afterward; or suggest you wait six months, work with your child and then return for another try, or say he or she will represent your child on a trial basis (meaning the agent is not real excited, but does see potential and wants to give it a try for a while). Don't rely on just one person's opinion, especially if this is the child's first interview. Try a few more agents and see how it goes. Your child may do a better job the next time out. And while one agent may be just a little interested, another may be very enthusiastic. However, if you get a similar response from several agents, such as suggestions to attend a workshop or wait awhile, then you should follow their advice. This is their profession, after all—their business, how they make a living. They do know what they are talking about. Your odds of forcing a child into working when he is not ready are *zero*. Don't try it. It's not fair to the child.

But what if you get the response you want to hear: an enthusiastic "Yes, we'd like to represent Samantha. She's a real character." That's great news. Your practice has paid off and you've passed the first major hurdle. But . . . it's just the beginning. There are several things you can do to improve your child's chances of working and to maintain a good relationship with your agent. The agent will probably not have the time to sit down and go over in detail what's expected and things for you to do. Here is a list of the basics:

1. Abilities: Your child doesn't have to be an expert at everything, but the more activities he has a working knowledge of, the better the opportunities. Things like skating, swimming, jumping rope, playing basketball, skateboarding, etc., all help. Your new agent will have you complete a detailed information sheet for the agency's use. (See the Sample Agency Information Sheet on page 44.)

2. Phone Numbers: Give the agency a list of numbers where you can be reached—work, home, emergency. Get an answering machine and *check it* often.

3. Travel: If you're going out of town, or on vacation, notify your agent when and for how long.

4. Unavailable: Let your agent know if you are not going to be available, even if for only one day. Agents are often working several days ahead on scheduling auditions. They should know in advance if you are not going to be available on a certain day.

5. Auditions: Keep the appointments. Don't miss them

Sample Agency Information Sheet

Name Jessica McDonald   Phone _____

Address _____   Phone _____

City _____ State _____ Zip _____   Emergency # _____

Social Security Number ___ ___ ___ Age _____ Birthdate 07/27/87

Height _____ Weight _____ Hair brown Eyes brown

Wardrobe Sizes: Shirt/Blouse _____ Pants _____ Shoes _____

Glasses? _____ Contacts? _____ Braces? ✓ Flipper? _____

Classes:

Singing _____ Dance _____

Acting _____

Other _____

Musical Instruments: _____

Language(s) English, Hebrew

Dialects _____

Check and rate (average, good, very good) the following if any experience:

✓Acrobatics good	Frisbee _____	Skateboarding _____
Archery _____	Golf _____	✓Skating—Ice good
Baseball _____	✓Gymnastics good	Roller good
Basketball _____	Hockey _____	Skiing—Snow _____
✓Bicycling average	Horseback Riding _____	Water _____
Billiards _____	Judo/Karate _____	✓Soccer very good
✓Bowling good	Juggling _____	Surfing _____
Boxing _____	✓Jumping Rope good	✓Swimming very good
✓Cheerleading good	Ping-Pong _____	✓Tennis average
✓Diving very good	Scuba _____	Volleyball _____

Describe any other skills or special abilities _____

_____

Date: _____ Parent's Name _____

except for illness or real emergencies. Treat this as a business. If you cannot make an audition, *let someone know*.

6. **Don't Pester the Agency:** Agents are busy and don't have time for idle chat. Contact them only when necessary.
7. **Pictures:** Keep the agency well supplied with up-to-date photos. If your agent calls and tells you he is running low and needs more pictures, get to the photo printing place right away.
8. **Work Permits:** Keep current . . . always. (More on this in the Working chapter.)
9. **Union Dues:** Keep current . . . always. (More on this in the Unions chapter.)
10. **Contracts, etc:** Do not sign anything if you are not sure of its meaning.

More detailed information on Auditions and Working is given in those chapters.

Okay, we've covered a lot of information so far. Let's do a quick review of what it will take to get started. First, the important questions:

1. Does your child really want to act in commercials?
2. Does your child honestly demonstrate enough of the right qualities?
3. Are you willing to persist and support your child?

If all your answers are Yes, keep going.

4. Make sure your child has a Social Security Number.
5. Get a list of agents.
6. Plan the pictures you are going to take: wardrobe, setting, props, etc.

7. Shoot at least two rolls of film, preferably in natural light.
8. Make copies of the picture(s) and mail to the agents along with an information sheet and introductory letter.
9. Practice "Agent Interview" at home.
10. Keep all appointments.

From getting a good agent or manager to landing a commercial or movie role, there's competition in the entertainment business, just like any other. But you can be sure that the ones who persist, who keep trying, are the ones who eventually come out ahead.

Three Important Things to Remember

1. It's your job to keep everything running as smoothly as possible, from work permits to joining the union. Your child has the responsibility of doing the best he can, from auditions to working.
2. Be supportive of your child. Encourage him in the job he is doing. Tell him how good he is and how proud you are of him every chance you get.
3. *Keep it fun!* Enjoy the experience. Your child will do better and so will you.

7

PERSONAL MANAGEMENT

Working with a management company is a personal choice. You are not required to do so. Many people, however, do find that working with a good, well-established manager is the best way to go—especially if new to the business. A manager can provide years of valuable experience which can greatly help your child's career and generally make things go much smoother. A considerable amount of what you are learning in this book can be taken care of by a manager.

The actual—or legal—job definition of a personal manager is "to advise and counsel." Under that description will fall numerous activities, but a personal manager's overall goal is to ensure that his or her clients are well qualified, have good representation, and are consistently auditioning for the roles they are right for. The duties a manager will perform depend greatly on the individual client and that client's status within the industry. For example, the work done for a young actor who has been in the business for several years and has a long list of credits (commercials, acting jobs, etc.) will be very different from the work done for a youngster who is just starting out. The veteran actor may require very important career and business advice regarding agency representation, publicity, current training recommendations, scheduling, finances, whether or not to accept a certain project, etc.

If a young actor is new to the business, then the first task a manager will concentrate on is preparing the child *and* the parents for getting started. This alone may take several weeks and will usually include personal coaching of the child in basic commercial audition technique and how to do well at an agent interview. Once the child is ready, the manager will set up an appointment with a good agency. The manager will want to be sure that all clients are well prepared and will act in a professional manner.

Once a client is accepted by an agent, the manager will then, in most cases, work directly with the agency in scheduling auditions, jobs, and matters that pertain to the child's career. A good manager will also provide the parents with all the necessary information and procedures for auditioning, working, current rules and regulations, and the day-to-day activities of being in this business. Valuable tips and insights that usually take years of experience to discover and utilize properly are immediately available from the manager. A manager will also advise on photographers, wardrobe selection, training and acting classes, and general day-to-day decisions. A manager may provide personal coaching prior to auditioning for a major movie or television role, or arrange a session with a professional coach. A manager may pick up, deliver, or fax scripts and pictures. Most managers will assist parents in obtaining copies of their children's commercials. A manager is someone to turn to with problems and frustrations.

A manager may handle promotional activities such as press announcements, mailings, and involvement in celebrity charity events. It is the manager's job to run interference and to do most of the worrying.

It's possible for a good manager to take a bright, talented youngster right off the streets and in a very short time have that child auditioning for top national commercials and other projects. A good manager can basically run the show for you. All you have to do is listen and follow his or her directions.

A manager can also be helpful to someone who has been in show business for a while and feels stalled in his or her career. The manager may first have a talk with the actor's agent to get a feeling as to how strongly the agent believes in the actor. A change in representation may be needed. The manager may suggest new pictures or an acting coach, or determine that the actor needs a new direction, such as more stage experience or some work on student films. The manager often provides something as simple as encouragement.

Some people will say, "Why have a manager? I can do a lot of this myself and save the percentage he charges." That certainly is true for many people. The information in this book provides the new parent with *all* of the basic information to do just that. As stated earlier, personal management is *not* for everyone. You should be very careful in making this decision. You and your child can have a long successful career together without the services of a manager. But, for others, it is well worth the extra percentage a personal manager collects.

As is true for talent agencies, some managers are very good, others are just okay, and still others are less than adequate. Managers often get a bad reputation because they are not regulated. It is possible for someone without *real* professional knowledge and experience to print up a few cards and call himself a personal manager. The thought usually goes something like this: All I have to do is take on a bunch of clients, maybe help them get an agent, and then set back and wait for them to start landing a bunch of jobs and then collect my percentage. Well, that's way off the mark. And those who attempt it usually find themselves dropping the idea quickly. To be successful as a manager requires staying power, business sense, and a *professional attitude*. It is not unusual for managers (and agents) to work many, many months with some clients who never land a job. This, of course, equals nothing, zero, in the way of pay. Personal management is not a business that will be profitable in a couple of months' time.

Essentially, managers and agents are risking their time and energy on the speculation that each client will pay off somewhere down the line. It's not a bad deal for the actors and parents when you think about it. You pay nothing up front—no financial risk—and receive the experience, knowledge, and benefits of having professional individuals working for you and your child. When your child does work, then your manager and agent get paid. It's as simple as that. With this in mind, you can see why managers and agents must have high standards for quality talent.

If you decide to work with a manager, in the beginning or later, use the same guidelines as for seeking an agent. Once you have a reputable manager who is interested in a meeting, make sure you and your child are prepared. A manager could be even more picky than some agents, because a manager may carry a client list of only twenty to forty (some more, some less) actors. An agency may carry hundreds. That manager has to be as certain as possible that the relatively small number of clients he or she represents will eventually work.

8

AUDITIONS

I n most cases your agent will call you the day before a
commercial audition. This will give you time to prepare
your schedule and decide on wardrobe. But this is not
always the case, especially when things are very busy. It
is quite normal to receive a call around 11 A.M. for an audition
later that same day. Always be prepared. Don't leave things to
chance or guesswork. Auditioning is what all the preparation
has been leading up to.

When the agent calls, the conversation will go something
like this: "Hi, this is Kathryn from the ACME Talent Agency.
We have an audition for Thomas tomorrow afternoon. The
product is ABC Cat Food and your call time is 4:15. You'll be
going to Pacific Casting at 1111 Star Drive in Hollywood. The
casting director is Mary Smith. They're looking for rough-
and-tumble boys in play clothes. Age range is six to seven."
There may be more, there may be less. The agent may have
been told there is a lot of dialogue to learn on this one and

that your child will have plenty of time to study it. Repeat the information to the agent to be sure it is correct.

Important Auditioning Tips

1. Never assume your child knows what the product is. If it is a toy, he should know how it works and what it looks like. If it is a food product, he should have some idea as to how it tastes and smells. If you cannot show it to him, explain in detail. The more he understands about the product, the better he will do on the audition.

2. Plan to arrive fifteen to twenty minutes early so that you are not rushed and have time to practice the script.

3. Look for the Sign In sheet as soon as you arrive. There will be one for each audition.

4. If there is a script for your child to learn, it will usually be located next to the Sign In sheet. Depending on the length or difficulty of the script, you may want to delay signing in until your child has had time to practice. Otherwise, your child may be called in to the audition without being prepared.

5. Record each audition in a calendar book. Make notes of who, what, when, where, and wardrobe used. This information will be useful at later dates.

6. On call-backs (unless otherwise requested), return in the same wardrobe and hairstyle as the first call, because whatever they liked the first time, you want to repeat it. Refer to your calendar book if you cannot recall what your child wore the first time.

7. Always carry a photo to each audition. For theatrical calls, a current résumé should be attached to the back

of the photo. The résumé is not needed for commercial calls. The photo is given to the casting person when your child's name is called. If you are new to the business and do not have professional photos yet, bring a snapshot from home (maybe the same one used to get the agent interview). Write your child's name and agency on the back.

8. The actor should never feel rushed or put under extra stress.

9. During school time, all auditions for children of legal school age will be after school hours. Babies and preschool children can be given interviews late morning or early afternoon.

10. If your child has not done a commercial workshop, explain to him what is going to take place.

11. Many parents find it helpful to have a sports bag or small suitcase packed and ready to go at all times. This contains all the extras you may need from time to time: comb and brush, washcloth, water bottle, pictures and résumés, an extra shirt or blouse, snack foods, books and puzzles to occupy the time in case of a long wait, flippers (false teeth), etc.

12. Always notify your agent (or manager) if you cannot make it to an audition.

13. After the audition is complete, sign out and leave unless asked to wait.

14. Get a good map book and use it. Your agent doesn't have the time to give you directions from your home to the casting location. The same casting facilities are used over and over, so it won't take long to learn where most of them are.

15. A piece of tape is normally placed on the floor in the audition room several feet in front of the video

camera. This is called a marker and is the spot where your child will stand.

16. Your child should be prepared to do the audition alone, or with an adult or other children.

Commercial Coaching Tips

1. Look the script over. Describe what is taking place in the commercial. Talk about it with your child, especially if he is not reading yet. "Okay, this is a cat food commercial with two kids in it. You're going to be the younger brother. It looks like the two of you are standing in the backyard getting ready to feed the cat."

2. Make sure your child clearly understands all words in the script, even the ones that seem obvious. The better his understanding of the scene, the product, and the words, the better the audition will go.

3. Help your child learn the lines without showing how to do it. Don't demonstrate in your words and emotions. It has to come from the child. Coach by using key words and phrases: "Say it like you're real surprised," or "say the word *yummy* like you've just taken a bite of the best cake you've ever tasted."

4. Slating: In movie terms, the slate (also called a clacker) is a small blackboard that shows what scene and take are being shot. It is placed in front of the camera just as filming begins. For purposes of commercial auditions, the slate is an introduction. It means the actor should say his name and age: "Hi, my name is Thomas Smith and I'm seven years old." The slate begins all commercial auditions. Sometimes, that *is* the audition. It must be bright, natural, and convey an "I'm glad to be here" feeling.

5. Watch for wiggling and wasted motion. Movement of the hands and body should have something to do with the audition.
6. Your child's voice should be clear and louder than normal. Eye contact should be with the camera.
7. Your child should look *at* the camera during the audition.
8. Your child must listen to the directions of the casting person. He or she will tell the actor what is wanted. It's okay to ask questions if the scene or dialogue is confusing.
9. The child should not be thrown off by mistakes—his own, or others'. He should stay in character and continue.

What Not to Do at an Audition

1. Do not bring relatives, friends, or extra kids. The rule is "one parent, one child." This rule also applies to working.
2. Do not chew gum.
3. Don't tell your child there is something wrong with his appearance, clothing, or attitude.
4. Do not let your child bother other children.
5. Do not bring a child who is ill.
6. Do not chastise your child in the waiting room.
7. Don't ask the casting director questions like "How did Tommy do?" or "Did you like my little girl?"
8. Do not bring noisy or distracting toys to the waiting room.

Baby Auditions

The basic procedure is the same. Bring a picture with the baby's name and agency written on the back; sign in and wait to be called. As with the older children, each audition will be different. Sometimes it's just a look, or a match to an adult. They may give the baby a stuffed toy to play with or just call the baby's name to get a reaction. They may ask the parent to be involved in the audition by trying to get the baby to do something cute or unusual. Baby auditions are also put on videotape. A few tips:

1. Arrive early and take your time going inside. Give your baby a few minutes to wake up if he has fallen asleep on the way there. He should be happy and alert.
2. Make sure he is not hungry.
3. Try to avoid other babies in the waiting room if they are crying.

After an Audition

In most cases, the audition will be held behind closed doors so you will have to ask your child how he thinks things went in there. The temptation, of course, is to want to know every little detail, and kids being kids, they may not want to provide that. It's rather like asking your child how things went at school one day. More than likely, the response you get will be along the lines of a mumbled "Fine." That may be all you'll get from your child after the audition. Other times, you may get a complete rundown. As frustrating as it is, you're going to have to go with what you get. Don't pester your child. Besides, most of the time your parental instincts will be able to determine how the audition went.

Don't hesitate to compliment and reward your child for doing a good job on the auditions. Let him know how proud you are. Auditioning can be hard work and your child is probably doing the best he can. Don't show disapproval or disappointment. Encouragement builds confidence; confidence leads to better auditions. And never tell your child you think he did or did not get the job. It's almost impossible to predict.

Since not every child is qualified for or has the right look for every job, don't be offended if your child does not go out on a particular call. In other words, a young boy who has a blond, Southern California surfer look may not get the call for an East Coast bank commercial. And vice versa. It is the agent's job to determine which child is right for which job.

Don't panic if your child goes out on several auditions without picking up a job—especially if he's new at audition-ing. Occasionally a child will land a job the first or second time out, but that is very rare. Persist, persist, persist. Your child will improve and gain confidence each time out. The day will come when everything clicks together: the right look, personality, good dialogue—and you've landed your first job.

Now, let's review the steps of that first audition:

1. Your agent calls with the information.
2. You double-check that your child knows what the product is and make your scheduling arrangements.
3. Arrive early, look for any dialogue scripts, and sign in.
4. The casting person will call your child's name off the list and ask him to step into the audition room.
5. Your child will hand his picture to the casting person on the way in.
6. The audition is completed; you sign out and leave.

Call-backs

After the first audition, approximately three-fourths of the children will be eliminated. The remainder will be "called back" for another look. This is done in order to make the final selection easier. Almost all auditions have at least one call-back, sometimes more. Call-backs should *always* be considered positive—even if your child does not land the job. It shows he was in the running. Agents will take note of this. More call-backs will generally mean more auditions from the agent, which mean greater chances for working.

To Repeat: The most important point to remember for call-backs is to *always . . . always* return wearing the same wardrobe (and hairstyle) that was worn on the first call, unless otherwise requested. A call-back means that your child performed well on the audition. You don't want to change a thing at this point. The call-back will usually take place within seven to ten days after the first call. If you have forgotten what your child wore on that day, refer to your audition notebook.

Commercial Auditions versus Theatrical Auditions

The people who make commercials are looking for *natural,* spontaneous children. They want the actors doing dialogue to be just "kids," as if they were talking to friends or family. In other words, they don't want a perfect, polished performance . . . just something *real.* Sometimes there will be no dialogue or words spoken at all—it is simply a "look," or a match-up to create a "real family" look. There are exceptions, of course. Occasionally a role in a commercial may call for the child to perform in an outlandish or unusual way. But that is rare. In most cases, the real-kid image is what is wanted.

Theatrical auditions give the child an opportunity to act. He may have to "cold-read" a script (pick up a script, study it for a few minutes, and then do the audition). This is where talent is important, the ability to show different emotions convincingly and to improvise on the spot. It is one thing to be able to say a few lines for a thirty-second commercial and quite another to act for a half-hour sit-com or be a co-star in a feature-length film. The acting may require the ability to memorize long, complicated lines and to change emotion several times throughout the project. In most cases, a good acting class taught by a professional coach is important to your child's development in the theatrical side of the business.

As a general rule, fewer children are called for theatrical auditions than for commercials. This is because the casting directors usually want to see only the most skilled children and therefore request fewer children from the agents.

The audition itself is similar to a commercial call: Bring a photo (and résumé), study the script, sign in, do the audition, sign out. The script (known as "sides"—a portion of the script to be used on the audition) is usually available before the audition and can be picked up and studied in advance. Cameras are rarely used on theatrical calls, especially the first one. Call-backs may be conducted on camera. A first call for a theatrical role may not involve any scripts or acting ability. It may be simply a meeting with the casting director. If he or she is interested after that, the child will be given a script and asked to return.

Cattle Calls

Cattle calls are mostly a thing of the past and not something to worry about. That's not to say you won't attend some auditions under crowded circumstances, and you will have the occasional long wait, but strict union rules on the amount of time an actor can spend at a commercial audition without being paid limits how many people may be called at once.

An "open call" is what it says: open to the public. Attending one of these auditions is a real shot in the dark. Hundreds and sometimes thousands of would-be actors for miles around can, and do, show up. Open calls are sometimes used as a promotional gimmick to bring attention to a project. In most cases, they are a waste of time and not seriously considered by agents.

9

WARDROBE

The choice of wardrobe for each audition *is* important but, at the same time, should be a relatively simple decision to make. It is easy to get too concerned about clothing and make the common mistake of overdoing it. This is especially true of people new to the business. Walk into the waiting room of a casting office and it's not too difficult to spot the kids who are on one of their first auditions. They will tend to stand out because they are overdressed. The boys will usually look *too* neat and polished, with every hair in place. The girls probably will look as if they stopped off on the way to a beauty pageant.

Normal everyday play clothes are the most popular and frequently requested form of clothing. The term *casual* or *cute/casual* is often used to describe the appropriate look on a commercial audition. Once again, keep in mind: Real kids doing real things. This will generally describe most commercials using children. Of course, use a little common sense.

"Real kids doing real things" does not mean you should bring little six-year-old Jimmy to an audition with matted hair, dirty hands, and covered in playground dust.

Perhaps the best examples of what type of clothing to use can be discovered by watching television. Sit down and take a few notes. Observe what the kids are wearing in the majority of the spots. Unless it is a very specific type of commercial—e.g., little boys wearing cowboy clothes for a dog food commercial, or young girls dressed as dancers—you will notice the kids are generally dressed in regular, everyday-type clothes.

When in doubt as to what clothing to dress your child in, always lean toward the "less is best" principle.

The above is true unless a specific type is *requested*. Examples would be: athletic, tomboy, preppie, Southern California, country, hip or trendy, and street tough, or variations of each. The request could be very exact.

For example, the casting director might say, "We are looking for a tough, young James Dean type, ten to twelve, in this ad. We would like to see all the boys dressed in old, faded jeans, T-shirt, and Levi jacket or something similar. Please comb hair appropriately."

Or the casting director might say, "This spot calls for a very trendy, very off-the-wall kind of look. The girls should dress really wild, show what's popular with the early teens on the streets of Los Angeles."

The requests above are not your average, everyday calls, but they give you an idea of what might be asked for. Most of what you will need for auditioning can probably be found in your child's current wardrobe. A few added bits here and there and you're all set. Once you get rolling and you find you are going on lots of auditions, start adding anything that might come in handy for the requested spots. Go to your local thrift store and browse around. Pick up a pair of suspenders, an odd hat or two, an old letter jacket, or faded overalls. Don't spend a lot of money on these things. You may never use them, but they're handy to have around.

Suggestions for a Typical Commercial Audition

Boys

1. Jeans and athletic shirt, such as a football jersey.
2. Jeans and T-shirt or plaid shirt.
3. Shorts, T-shirt, and sneakers are fine, especially in warm weather.
4. School slacks and button-down shirt or pullover.
5. Overalls and T-shirt for younger boys.

Girls

1. Simple play dress or jumper with sneakers or sandals.
2. Jeans, T-shirt, sneakers, maybe suspenders.
3. Shorts, T-shirt or blouse, and kneesocks.
4. Cute overalls with a simple blouse for younger girls.

Babies

Select clothing that best shows a *baby*, not a small child. Use bib overalls, T-shirt and shorts, or a sleeper—all in nice fun colors. Choose outfits that are easily removed in case the casting director needs to see the baby in diapers.

Additional Notes Regarding Wardrobe

1. After several auditions, you will find that one or two outfits will work on the majority of the calls. Consider

those as "first choice"—especially if your child gets call-backs or jobs while wearing them.

2. Always have these clothes clean and ready to go.
3. Avoid splashy or busy patterns—polka dots and conflicting lines of color. Do not use T-shirts with writing or large pictures on the front. They are very distracting.
4. Follow your agent's advice. Ask if there is a special look.

Prepare yourself for those times when you walk into a casting office and find that all the kids look as if they just walked in from the farmyard; every kid except yours. It happens. Someone goofed and you didn't get the requested look for that commercial. Don't worry about it; go ahead and do the audition. Next time, it will be someone else. Besides, your child could still land the job. The wardrobe is important, but it's still just part of the packaging.

What to Avoid on Most Auditions Unless Requested

Girls

Frilly dresses, large bows and ribbons, petticoats, high heels, heavy makeup, sophisticated hairstyles, boots, very trendy clothing. Jewelry should be limited to a very basic necklace and bracelet. Very simple earrings are okay on older girls.

Boys

Dress suits, jogging suits, athletic uniforms, tank tops, distracting hats, very trendy clothing.

Babies

Turtlenecks, frilly dresses, large hats and bonnets, headbands and earrings.

Colors

Select colors that are becoming to your child's hair, eye, and skin color. Colors should enhance facial features, not distract or make a child look sallow or pale. Almost all commercial auditions are shot on video camera for viewing at a later time. Some colors—usually blacks, mustard yellows, some browns, too much white and beige—do not look good on video. Since one color may work well for one child and not another, it is an excellent idea to experiment with a video camera at home to determine which colors and outfits are most complimentary to your child.

A Few Tips on Hair

Boys

Hair should be neat, but not so neat that it looks as if every hair is perfectly in place. It should look natural and be the length of the current styles.

Girls

The best styles are generally the more traditional ones. If hair is worn long and hanging down, make sure it doesn't distract your daughter's attention by hanging around her face.

The Final Word on Wardrobe

Keep in mind that commercials using kids are usually trying to reach a broad audience—they want to produce something the average viewer can relate to. Green hair, mismatched shoes, and clothes worn inside out may indeed be popular where your child is going to school, but just won't cut it for a commercial trying to reach an audience in the millions. Stick with the everyday normal . . . unless requested.

10

WORKING

J ust when you were beginning to wonder if the scheduling changes, the last-minute calls, all those trips to the casting offices during rush-hour traffic were ever going to pay off—you get the call you've been waiting for: "Congratulations, Thomas is booked on the cat food spot."

But . . . let's back up just a bit. The first call you may get regarding that job is something known as an "availability." In other words, the casting office has called your agent and has asked that your child be made "available" on a particular date for a possible booking. That's good news. Most of the time, an availability turns into a booking. But sometimes not. So save your celebration until you hear the words, "He's booked." That's the time to jump on the phone to notify your friends, neighbors, relatives, and especially anyone who was negative enough to tell you it would never happen.

So now, let's take a look at exactly what a booking, or getting a job, means.

The Work Permit and Regulations

Strict rules and regulations regarding minors working in the entertainment industry will vary from state to state. You should check with your nearest union office—that's the Screen Actors Guild (SAG) or the American Federation of Television and Radio Artists (AFTRA)—or the state Labor Board for the correct information in your area. Most of the information contained in this book pertains to union rules and California laws.

The job your child will be working on will be either union or nonunion. If it is a nonunion job, the state's child labor laws will still be in effect. Union jobs and their rules regarding minors will take precedence over any state laws if those state laws are less restrictive. If a minor, who is a resident in the state of California, is hired by an employer also located in California, then all child labor laws pertaining to California are applicable on any location outside of the state.

In California, a current entertainment work permit is the first thing asked for upon arrival on the set. Make no mistake about it: No work permit, no work! Babies included. This of course is for your child's protection. Minors in California are required to file an application to work in the entertainment industry. This is done through the nearest state Labor Board. The Labor Board will provide an application to be filled out by the parent on the front side. The reverse side is completed by the child's school. Attendance and grades are looked at. Too many absences or any grades falling below satisfactory and the permit cannot be granted. If the child is not yet in school, the school side is left blank. Birth certificates are required in all cases.

There is some leeway in an emergency. A temporary permit may be granted if school is not in session and no one is available from the school. Bring the child's last report card and a completed application to the job.

The work permit is good for six months and then must be renewed. This is left up to the parents. Don't expect anyone to remind you. Each time you receive a new permit, mark the renewal date in your calendar book. Don't let it lapse—even for a couple of days. You just never know. The oddest things can happen in this business. You may suddenly get a call telling you your child is booked on something he had auditioned for weeks earlier. Or maybe your child is called in at the last minute because the first child hired came down with the flu and couldn't work.

Teacher/Welfare Worker

This person is a teacher who holds a current state teaching credential and is provided by the producer to supervise and teach. She or he is on the work set to ensure that all rules and regulations governing the employment of minors are enforced and will also act as the tutor for the children during times they would normally be in school. This is the person to turn to if you have any questions regarding your child and working regulations.

It is your responsibility to contact your child's teacher the day before working and bring homework and lesson plans to the set.

Wardrobe Call

Prior to working, you will be contacted by your agency or the production company. A wardrobe call may be requested prior to working. This is an appointment to try on the clothes for the job. It is possible that someone from the production company filming the commercial will want to see a selection of your child's wardrobe as well as the clothes the producers have. Do not feel obligated to buy anything if you do have the type of thing they request. If your child does wear his clothes during the filming of the commercial, he will be paid a separate fee for doing so.

Not every job has a separate wardrobe call. The person responsible for wardrobe selection may ask for a list of your child's sizes ahead of time and will have the appropriate clothing when your child arrives on the set.

Your child will also be paid a separate amount if he does attend a wardrobe call. Your agent or union can quote the current fees for use of wardrobe and a wardrobe call.

Call Time and Location

Your agent, manager, or someone from the production company will call to let you know when and where the job is going to be. You may not be given this information until late the day before. Don't panic! Someone will contact you. Just be sure you can be reached the day before your child works in case of any last-minute changes.

Guardians

When a minor is working, a parent or guardian *must* be present. That person must also be within sight or sound of the minor. A guardian is defined as someone eighteen years or older. A parent may authorize (in writing) another person to act as the child's guardian for the day. Included with the authorization should be the parent's phone number, doctor's phone number, and any specific medical or nutritional information concerning the child.

Important Working Tips

1. Bring current work permit and two forms of I.D.
2. Plan to arrive early and allow for traffic.
3. Bring wardrobe if requested to do so.
4. Bring homework for the set teacher.
5. Bring any special medication or dietary needs.
6. Let the teacher/welfare worker know you have arrived.
7. Report problems or complaints to the teacher/welfare worker.
8. If you are shooting on location, a catered lunch will be served. Otherwise, be prepared with money for lunch or bring your own.
9. Do not bring relatives, friends, or other children (the one parent, one child rule).
10. Do not leave the set.
11. Do not interrupt the classroom.
12. Do not tell your child what to do in front of the camera. That is the director's job.
13. If someone is acting as the guardian for the day, make sure that person has a permission slip authorizing him or her to do so.
14. Call your agent or manager if you have any questions not being resolved on the set.
15. Check in with your manager or agent to see if there are any auditions scheduled for after the job.
16. Bring a book or something to entertain yourself. It can be a long day for the parent.
17. You and your child are expected to conduct yourselves in a professional manner.

What Your Child Can Expect When He Works

Before your child works on his first job, it is very helpful to prepare him for what might occur on the set. The following will give you a general idea:

1. To be asked to repeat or do the same thing over and over. It is not uncommon for a scene to be repeated twenty or thirty times to get it right. And that is not to say your child is doing it incorrectly. There are dozens of small details that must all come together to get the shot right.
2. To have the mandatory three-hour school time on the set cut into segments—one hour of school, one hour in front of the camera, etc.
3. Several changes in and out of wardrobe.
4. Long periods of waiting. There are many activities and changes that take place during the filming of a commercial or movie. Sometimes a whole new set needs to be built on the spot, or technical difficulties with the equipment or props occur, or the sun or weather is not right. This is why a thirty-second commercial can take all day to shoot.
5. To repeat: Your child will be expected to act like a professional. This means listening and following directions. The same applies to the parent or guardian. Hollywood brats and stage parents are not welcome on any set.

Getting a job is the end result of all your hard work. Enjoy the experience. It should be fun. Pay attention to what is going on, ask questions if you do not understand something, and know what your rights are. Just as your child should act responsibly, so should you. You and your child are there to get a job done. There is a lot of work and money involved. Once you have done two or three jobs, you will begin to notice that the actual process is much the same from one to the next— different products, different locations, etc., but essentially the same procedure for each commercial.

Hours of Work

The number of hours a child may work is determined by two sources: the state child labor laws and the union. The age of the child and schooling are also taken into consideration. The table on the opposite page shows the current working hours for minors in California. Check with your local union or state Labor Board for details in your area.

Contracts

(The following is repeated from a previous section of this book. It is added here as an important reminder.) The work referred to in this book pertains primarily to union—SAG and AFTRA—jobs. The majority of all commercials seen on TV, especially major spots playing to a national audience, are filmed under the contractual agreements of one of the unions. The majority of all roles cast in television programs and motion pictures are union. Nonunion jobs are, in most cases, lower-budget productions. They do not have to adhere to the strict union rules regarding working and auditioning or any particular pay scale or overtime hours, and are not under any obligation to provide certain amenities, such as a catered lunch on location. They do, however, have to abide by all state rules and regulations governing the employment of minors.

Working Hours of Minors in California

Ages	Time on Set	Time at Work	School	Rest and Recreation	Total Time Includes Meal
15 days through 5 months	2 hours	20 minutes		1 hour, 40 minutes	2½ hours
6 months through 1 year	4 hours	2 hours		2 hours	4½ hours
2 years through 5 years	6 hours	3 hours		3 hours	6½ hours
6 years through 8 years	8 hours	4 hours	3 hours	1 hour	8½ hours
		6 hours	vacation	2 hours	
9 years through 15 years	9 hours	5 hours	3 hours	1 hour	9½ hours
		7 hours	vacation	2 hours	
16 and 17 years	10 hours	6 hours	3 hours	1 hour	10½ hours
		8 hours	vacation or graduation	2 hours	

There will be a job contract for you to sign the day your child works. The contracts for commercial employment are essentially the same from one job to the next, but it is still something you should discuss with your agent or manager before going to the job.

Here are a few basics to be aware of:

1. Classification

    Actor/actress or player
    On Camera
    Off Camera

If child is "on camera," he is also known as a principal performer. Extras are "off camera" and are seen in the background only.

2. Salary. Listed as *session fee:* the standard amount for a day's work on a commercial; currently $414.25 per day excluding overtime.

3. Wardrobe Fee. If your child used his own clothing for the commercial, then a fee is to be paid. This should be indicated on the contract.

4. Where Payments Are to Be Mailed

   a. To Performer _____(address)_____

   b. To Performer c/o Agent _____(address)_____

   The above are the two choices given to you on your job contract. The normal procedure is for the checks to be mailed to the agent first. The agent will take the proper commission (10% of the gross) and reissue a check to your child in his name. You will receive full verification of all amounts received by the agent and the commission and taxes taken out.

5. Signing Contracts. The parent or legal guardian is responsible for signing contracts.

6. Form W-4. Usually attached to contract.

   a. Use child's social security number.
   b. It is advisable to check with an accountant or tax professional in advance to determine the proper way to fill out this form for your situation.

If you are ever handed a contract that does not correspond to what your agent has told you, or if anything has been added or is missing, or if you have any questions at all—call your agent or manager before signing.

11

MONEY

pproximately three to four weeks after work done on a commercial, the actor will receive a payment known as a "session fee." This payment covers the time spent on the set and will include any wardrobe and overtime fees that may be due. The basic session fee amount (currently $414.25) does not vary on union jobs. That is the flat rate paid to all actors. The actor does not actually have to be in front of the camera working. He could be rehearsing lines, studying in the classroom, trying on wardrobe, or just relaxing. The age of the actor and number of hours spent on the set does not influence that basic amount, either. A child who falls into the two- to five-year-old age bracket can spend a maximum of six and a half hours on the set. His rate for a day on a commercial set is $414.25—the same rate that is paid to a six- to eight-year-old whose maximum time on the set is eight and a half hours. That same rate holds true for babies and teenagers. (See the Working chapter for a complete breakdown of age and allowable work hours.) Any time spent beyond their standard maximum allowable hours will fall into the overtime category.

It is customary for the agency to receive payments for their clients. The agency will process the check and send a new check to the actor—minus its commission—from the agency account. In the case of a basic session fee check, the agency's commission will be $41.42, ten percent of $414.25. So the actor will receive $372.83. Along with the check will be a pay sheet providing information about the money and the job. Some of the data included on that pay sheet:

1. Advertising agency/production company
2. Commercial I.D. number
3. Name of the company advertising
4. The product
5. Title of commercial
6. What the check is for (why you are being paid)
7. Taxes
8. Year-to-date earnings
9. Other information

These pay sheets should be filed and kept in a safe place. They will provide you with ongoing information about the commercial. Should you have any questions about the job, call the bookkeeper at your agency.

Your child can be paid under several different categories on one commercial. There are: session fees, holding fees, class A use, wild spots, cable broadcast, and others. In almost all cases, you will have little or no idea as to how much a commercial will eventually earn. It can get quite complicated. Time of day it is shown, what cities, whether it's cable or network, how many times aired . . . these are a few of the factors involved. Payments received as a result of filmed or taped material are called "residuals." There are different pay scales applied to each category a commercial may be running in, from sliding scales to number of unit weights designated to each city. One commercial may have a nice little run and earn a few thousand dollars. Another may saturate the airwaves and play for months and months, eventually bringing in many thousands and thousands of dollars.

(Note: A nonunion job will rarely—almost never—have an arrangement of residual payments. It is a one-time, flat-rate fee for the actor's time on the day of shooting.)

One payment category you should be familiar with is the "holding fee." When someone shoots a commercial—say it's for a soft drink—that person is then "held" or blocked from shooting a commercial for a competing product, in this case, another soft drink company. The actor is paid a holding fee to not audition for competing spots. This is done until the actor is "released." There are time limitations and other considerations concerning this fee, so once again, call your agent if you have any questions.

Your Child's Money and the Law

The California Civil Code contains a law that, under certain conditions, protects the earnings of a minor. This law is usually referred to as the "Jackie Coogan Law." This law affects money earned while a child is under a contract that has been heard by the court. A producer may take a child's contract before the courts to have it affirmed. Unless the contract is made valid by a judge, a minor can refuse to abide by it. In the process of affirming the contract, the court will order a percentage of the monies to be put into a blocked trust. The amount ordered will vary. This procedure is not in effect in all states, but some have similar laws regarding the earnings of children. It would be wise to check your state's Department of

Labor for the exact information appropriate for your situation. Your agent should also be able to guide you to the proper source.

In the case of commercials or smaller theatrical roles, the process of affirming the contracts through the courts is *usually* not done. That does not mean never, but very, very rarely. Contracts regarding major roles in TV series or feature films that require longer time commitments are the projects most often taken before the courts.

This means that the money your child will earn doing commercials and bit parts will not be required by law to be set aside into any sort of a blocked account. After the agent's commission, the remainder will be sent directly to your child in his name.

And this is where the whole concept of children working in this business can get very touchy. The terrible stories of child stars working for years, earning in some cases small fortunes, only to discover later on that the money had been spent by greedy parents are well documented. As in most any other activity or profession, a small number can have the effect of making everyone look bad—or suspicious.

So, let's set the record straight here. *Most* parents do not help their kids begin a career in commercials or motion pictures in order to live off their children's earnings. *Most* parents are not stage-struck, money-grubbing ogres. *Most* parents would pull their kids from this business in an instant if they thought the child was being taken advantage of in any way. A few bad apples? Sure, they exist. So what? They have nothing to do with most parents who are putting in a lot of time and real effort—and, in the beginning, out-of-pocket expense— into their child's career in the hopes that the income will help pay for private school, or college, or some other activity they may otherwise never be able to afford, or maybe just provide a nice investment for the child to start off on an independent life once he leaves home.

That's what most parents are interested in when it comes to the money side of this business. That's what most parents reading this book are interested in. You should not feel guilty or ashamed or afraid of what someone else may think. You and your child are probably going to work very hard to get to the point where some money begins to come in. And when that time does come, you should feel proud of your achievement.

Running Your Child's Career as a Business

That heading may sound a bit harsh, but it's important for you to understand that a child working in this field *should* be considered as a business and it will be wise for you to approach it that way. *Before* your child begins to work and the checks start arriving, you should think about what to do with the money and about that all-time favorite, *taxes!* Some parents make the mistake of doing nothing with the money. In other words, they may be so afraid of being accused of doing something wrong with their child's money that they may do something even worse . . . ignore it!

As with any business, your child's business will have expenses and taxes to pay. It is a good idea to employ a tax accountant—one who is knowledgeable in this field—prior to that first job. Let that person guide you to make proper basic decisions that will benefit your family. Things can change rapidly in this business. If your child has a sudden jump in income, or suddenly lands six commercials in a row, it would again be wise to seek further tax assistance at that point.

Numerous deductions are available. *Always* consult with your accountant if questions arise, especially if your child has high earnings.

The following list gives many of the items that *may* be deductible. It is not intended as an exact guide, nor will it apply to all situations; it is only a reference.

Acting class tuition
Commercial class tuition
Phone out of pocket
Agent's commission
Trade publications
Mileage for auditions
Pager
Postage
Parking
Pictures
Manager's commission
Union dues
Photocopying
Public relations

Use the list above as a general guide in keeping accurate records. A good rule of thumb is to keep records and receipts for everything even remotely related to this business. Toss them all in an envelope or shoe box. You probably won't need them all . . . but then again. . . .

Another suggestion is to open a simple checking account in your child's name. Bank policies vary on this, so you should explain to your bank representative what you want to do. Treat this personal checking account as a "business" checking account. Deposit all checks sent to your child into this account and distribute the funds from there.

For example: A check arrives in the amount of $1,200. The agent's commission and taxes have already been taken out. If you have an arrangement with your child that he receive a small payment,—say $25—then that amount might be paid to him in cash. Looking over your notes, you see that upcoming expenses include tuition for an important acting class. That's going to run $175. And pictures are getting low, so you'll need to order more, at the cost of $100. Those three items add up to $300, so you leave $350 (a little extra for unexpected expenses) in the account to cover those immediate expenses and write a check for the remainder—$850—to your child's savings or investment account.

What you've done in this example is to pay your child, set money aside for expenses so that they do not come out of your pocket, and deposited the remainder into the savings account. The expenses are tax deductible for your child. The next check may be distributed in an entirely different manner. Perhaps the entire amount will go to the savings account. By running the checks through a central system, you will have an accurate record of all money in and all money out.

The information above is simply intended to give you a few ideas for handling your child's money. Each family and each situation is different and demands its own approach. Some parents choose to pay all continuing expenses out of their own pockets and deposit all of their child's earnings into a trust or some other special account. Others will occasionally pay themselves a small parent/manager commission to cover their time and expenses. Those who do that should understand that any money they are paid is considered income by the IRS and will have to be reported as such.

Finally, perhaps the very best reason for keeping accurate and detailed records of your child's earnings is for that day several years from now when your child comes up to you and asks, "Can you show me what's happened to all the money I've made so far?"

12

HOW TO GET COPIES OF YOUR CHILD'S COMMERCIALS

E verything went as you hoped it would on the set. Your child did a great job and was the hit of the day. The director of the commercial even came up to you afterward and said he hoped to work with your child on another shoot in the near future. Now you can't wait to see the final result. Even more so, you can't wait for proud Grandma and Grandpa to witness what a talented grandchild they have.

Only one problem: How will that happen? What are the odds of everyone in the family spotting the commercial somewhere among fifty channels? Worse yet: What are the odds of your having the VCR set to record at the same moment the commercial flashes by? What if it plays only in some other part of the country? How will you get to see it?

Good questions, but don't worry. There are ways to handle this problem; listed below are three methods that will help.

    1. Request a Copy. Call the advertising company responsible for that commercial and ask to speak to someone in television traffic. Tell that person you would like to get a copy of a commercial your child did. Give them your child's name, the name of the product, the title of the commercial, the I.D. number, and the date it was filmed (this information is usually provided on the pay slip that accompanies all checks sent to your child). The response you receive regarding your request will vary from company to company. One may ask you to send a blank tape and they will copy the commercial onto it. Another may ask for your address and send one right out. Still another may charge a fee of anywhere from $25 to $65 for a copy.

2. **Record a Copy at Home.** Ask that same person in Television Traffic for something called "air dates." He or she should be able to tell you a few dates and programs that the commercial is scheduled to appear on. Call all the relatives and set the VCRs. This method, of course, is useful only if you live in the same area where the commercial will be showing.

The above methods are preferred, but they don't always work. It's possible to get someone who just doesn't want to bother with your request. Or it may be difficult to get hold of the person in charge of that department. Maybe your calls are not returned. Or the company policy may be to never give out copies or information about a particular commercial. Persistence will pay off in most cases, though.

If not, see step 3.

3. **Find and Record the Commercial Yourself.** This will require real persistence on your part, but it does work. First, recruit friends and relatives. Next, narrow the field of choice by determining which programs the commercial would *most likely* appear on. Example:

cereal products, toys, fast foods, and snack foods have a good chance of being seen on cartoon shows, after-school programs, and kid's specials. Another example: detergent, toothpaste, household cleaners, and diapers are more likely seen during midmorning and afternoon programs like game shows, talk shows, and soap operas. Tell your recruits what the commercial will look like and ask them to let you know if they spot it on one of the programs. If someone does see it, make sure you record that same program the following day or the next week. Odds are in your favor that it will show up there again.

If your child remains in the business for some time and shoots several commercials, it is doubtful that you will see them all. Cancellations, regional showings, and bureaucracy can present many problems. But if you stick with the methods detailed above, you'll get most of them.

13

UNIONS

 here are two unions you will be concerned with:

1. The Screen Actors Guild (SAG)—has jurisdiction over productions shot on film. Shares videotape responsibility with AFTRA in TV programming, TV commercials, and industrial/educational programs.
2. The American Federation of Television and Radio Artists (AFTRA)—has jurisdiction over work in live television, radio programs, and radio commercials and musical recordings.

There are branch offices of these unions across the United States. (See the listings at the end of this book.)

When Does Your Child Have to Join?

The majority of work available for your child—commercials, television series, motion pictures—will be through one of the unions, SAG or AFTRA. The potential employers have signed agreements with the unions stating, among other things, that they will comply with the regulations regarding employment of their members. It will be to your child's advantage to become a union member.

But your child *does not* have to be a member of any union to work that first job. This is where a federal regulation known as Taft-Hartley comes in. The Taft-Hartley regulation states that a person does not have to join a union until thirty days *after* the first job. He may work on other jobs during this thirty-day "grace" period. Once the thirty days have passed, he is obligated to join the union before working on the next job.

For example: On March 31, your child shoots a SAG commercial. Appropriate paperwork will be sent by your agent to the union making your child eligible to join. On May 20, your child gets hired for another commercial. The thirty-day grace period has passed, so he is now what is called a "must join," meaning he cannot work on that job until he becomes a member of the union.

So, in other words, your child is free to go out and get an agent, begin auditioning, and get hired on his first union job without having to pay any fees. Once he has become eligible, and the thirty-day grace period has passed, you have no choice but to join if you wish to continue doing union work. Note also that once you become a member of the union, you are not allowed to work on nonunion productions.

If your child works *prior* to the age of four, membership in the union is not required.

There is a one-time initiation fee to join the union. Yearly dues are paid after that. An orientation briefing will be given to all new members explaining the privileges and benefits of belonging to the union. Support your unions and take an active interest in what they are doing. The unions represent strength in bargaining for better working conditions and fair pay. For more information about benefits, credit unions, etc., contact your local union office.

14

THE PARENT'S ROLE

Often forgotten, but just as important as the desire and qualities of the child, are the responsibilities of the parent. In the entertainment business you will have the job of wearing two important and distinct hats: that of a parent and that of a parent/manager. How you wear these two hats will greatly determine your child's success and whether this will be an enjoyable experience—not only for the child, but for you and the rest of the family as well. Your primary concern, of course, is that of a parent. All of your duties and responsibilities as a parent should precede and direct your actions as a parent/manager.

Because you may be spending a great deal of extra time with your child, it is very important to keep the two areas separate. A verbal threat such as "Clean your room or I'm not taking you on the auditions" is a clear case of overlapping. Using the child's career in a threat would probably have only a negative effect. "Clean your room or no TV for a month" is more properly in line with your role as a parent.

The separation of hats for parents is obviously necessary, but your child also has a similar responsibility toward the business and will need to distinguish when you are wearing the Mom or Dad hat and when you are wearing the Parent/Manager hat. Mixing the two will only bring confusion. For example, your daughter should understand that when you are advising her to dress a certain way for an audition, you are doing so as her parent/manager. Your opinion in that capacity is important. Likewise, she should recognize that the request "to wash the dishes and feed the dog" comes from the parent.

It is similar to a husband and wife running a business together. If there is no agreement as to where to draw the line—separate the home life from the business life—then that couple may face added obstacles.

Parent/Manager Burnout and Other Problems

Communication is always the first step in dealing with problems. Talking to and listening to your child will resolve many of the difficult situations you may encounter. As an example, let's say that after a couple of successful years in the business, your child comes home from school one afternoon and suddenly announces, "I don't want to do commercials anymore. I'm tired of it." Now, before you panic or leap to the phone to tell your agent it's all over, your first response should be to find out exactly *why* and *how* your child reached this decision. Is he *really* tired of all the auditions? Of working? Does he feel like it's interfering with other things he would like to do? Did someone at school or at one of the auditions say something upsetting to him?

Kids being kids, he could easily jump to a conclusion, make

an abrupt decision to quit, and then just as easily change his mind a few days later. It may be something resolved by simply having a good talk. What you are trying to do in a situation like this is to determine the *best* solution—based on what your child *really* wants. Don't let your child make a quick, unfounded decision about dropping out if it is something he may regret later on. Handle it as you would if the same announcement had been made about Little League or the school band.

It is important you know at all times how your child feels about being involved in this business. A few questions now and then like "Are you still enjoying this? Everything going okay?" may catch minor problems before they develop into something larger. And, of course, children should never be working just for the sake of pleasing mom and dad. If it does come to the point (and more than likely, eventually it will) where it really is your child's desire to quit, then that's his decision and you have to abide by it. It is okay to take a break for a while. Give your agency a call and say that your child needs some time off. Most agents are very understanding about that sort of thing and will usually leave the door open. A few months later your child might be revitalized and ready for more auditions.

But what happens if *you* want to quit? You're beginning to feel completely burned out and think that if you go on one more audition, you're going to wind up as an extra in a Looney Tunes Cartoon. Or what if scheduling constraints are becoming almost too much to handle or job demands have increased? Those are tough situations and do frequently occur. Little Tommy is having a ball, loving every minute of it. He's making new friends and gaining confidence—not to mention a growing savings account. The idea of removing him from an activity he really enjoys is very troubling. What do you do? You can't ignore your own situation.

Once again, a good place to begin is by talking about it. Talk to your agent, or personal manager if you have one; or talk to a friend who has children in the business. Maybe you need a short break from the sometimes hectic pace of auditioning. Discuss that option with your child. Maybe you could enlist the help of a friend or relative to help out now and then. Your agent may suggest slowing things down for a while, maybe sending your child only on specific auditions. Or your agent might refer you to a professional interview driver. There *are* solutions for the parent "burnout" syndrome. Don't ignore it. If this does becomes a problem, then you will have to seek the best answer for you and your family.

Goals and Rewards

Ask yourself a few important questions: Why put in all the time and effort? What's the motivation? And if your child is old enough to understand such things, "what's in it for him?" Other than the fact that you are practically bursting with pride that your child has gotten an agent and gone on a few auditions, your idea of a long-term goal for your child's career might be something like "to have enough money in the bank to fully fund a college education." That's a fine goal, and more than likely one you are very interested in. But for a seven- or eight-year-old, that goal is probably a bit unreal. Kids do understand money at that age, and spending some of it on a new bicycle or computer game is more in line with what they would relate to. Of course, the bulk of the earnings should still go toward something more substantial in the future, but it is important not to neglect the present.

Other motivations for the kids can be something as simple as the joy and excitement of seeing themselves on TV, or meeting someone famous. And they do get a kick out of school friends asking for an autograph. A reminder of the goals can be especially important during those times when auditions are slow in coming or if your child has done several auditions without landing a job. This is where you step in and act as a cheerleader. Keep the goals alive and real. Talk about how much fun it will be when you're all sitting around the living room and suddenly see the commercial your child made a couple of months earlier.

It also doesn't hurt for your child to receive a little financial reward for the work he has been doing. Consider paying him a percentage or portion of the money he earns. That would mean that each time a check comes in, he could expect to receive a small payment—just like any other working person. Don't forget, he's the one doing the auditions and putting in all those hours in front of the camera. With no rewards now, he may lose interest, just as you would if you were in his shoes. Imagine working for the next two or three years and not receiving a dime of your earnings until ten or twelve years later. It would be realistic to consider that your enthusiasm would wane after a while.

Of course, the amount your child receives should be an individual matter and would also depend on his age. Start with a small amount and gradually build it up as he remains in the business and learns more about handling money. Going to extremes and giving your child *too* much of each check could be just as bad as no pay at all. Choose an amount or percentage you feel comfortable with. Discuss it with your child and give him detailed examples.

Two very positive results can occur from paying your child for each job:

    1. The child is rewarded now for his efforts. He learns the concept of producing a product or service and being rewarded (paid) for that. Not a bad lesson to learn at a young age.

2. The child also learns the valuable lesson of handling his own money—money earned.

Be prepared for what happens when he first begins receiving his money. There is an even chance he will waste a good portion of it on what you may consider as nothing more than junk. That's okay; it's his money. But with your guidance, you can show him a few alternatives, give him some ideas about what he could accomplish with the money he is making. As an example, let's say that Junior has a couple of commercials running on the air and based on the percentage you came up with, he is personally receiving $10 or $15 each time a check arrives. Certainly not a lot of money, but still a sizable sum for a youngster. You might suggest that the new skateboard or video game he has been wanting for some time could be his if he saved a few of those checks. Junior thinks that is a good idea and in a couple of months has the skateboard. (Besides, you can only buy so much "junk.") This is only an example, but in it, three positive results have occurred:

1. Junior has learned about saving and handling money.
2. Junior is rewarded with something that is real to him.
3. Junior has achieved his goal.

Money can be a touchy subject, especially when it involves a child earning it. This section is not intended in any way to tell you what is the "right" or "wrong" thing to do with any earnings your child may receive as a result of being in this business. They are only suggestions based on many years of experience.

A final recommendation is to openly discuss finances with your child. Don't assume that because he is only eight or nine years old, he is not interested or knowledgeable about the money aspect of this business. A kid who is sharp enough to get a good agent and work in commercials or movies is usually very aware of these things. Communicate, reward your child, and keep the goals in mind. The rest should fall into place.

15

WHAT DOES IT REALLY TAKE TO BE IN THIS BUSINESS?

Well, okay, sounds good so far," you say. "But I've seen the talk shows. I know there's more to it. What's it *really* like?"

All right, that's a fair question. Let's take another look at what you may have to deal with.

1. You are usually notified of auditions the day before, but many times you will be informed of a 4:00 P.M. audition at 11:30 A.M. the same day. That could call for a quick change in plans and a lot of hustle.

2. You may have two or even three auditions in one day. They may be spaced only thirty to forty minutes apart (or less) and you have to contend with a wardrobe change in the car and more driving across town in rush-hour traffic.

3. When school is in session, you have to be available every afternoon after school.

4. There is the "one parent, one child" rule. That means

that extra kids at the auditions are frowned upon. This also means sometimes getting hold of a sitter on short notice.

5. You have signed your child up for piano/dance/karate classes after school. Auditions interfere and you find yourself scrambling lesson schedules around.

6. If your son or daughter is going to auditions on a regular basis, it makes it very difficult to be involved in other activities requiring commitment. Your child can't betray the basketball or swimming team, and it's really not okay to turn down auditions.

7. Your child is on his second call-back for a big national commercial or movie role and it can get tense! If you're the nervous type, then this business may not be for you. Your anxiety won't help your child. You will have to learn to take it all in stride or get someone else to take your child to the auditions.

8. It's possible to go on many, many auditions, get a lot of call-backs, and *still* not land a job. Can you stick with it and keep your enthusiasm up?

9. Are you willing and able to put out money for pictures, classes, flippers, etc.? Not to mention the wear and tear on the family car.

10. Finally, after all those auditions, your child lands a job. He shoots the commercial, but for some reason they decide not to run it on the air. He still gets paid for his time working, but now you won't get to see it—*and* there will be no residuals!!

11. Sara really wanted to do this. You spend weeks getting her an agent and doing pictures. She takes an acting class and goes on numerous auditions. Just when it seems like she's starting to roll, she decides she would rather be a cheerleader.

12. Or . . . Sara's enthusiasm is just as great as it was when you started. She is considered a hot prospect by her agent. She is sent on every possible audition she is right for. Months go by—schedule changes, late dinners, waiting, traffic, waiting, last-minute calls, waiting—*your* enthusiasm begins to fade. You're supposed to be encouraging her, but who is encouraging you?

13. You just got a call for a theatrical audition. It's a good role for your child to audition for. But first, you'll have to make an extra trip to the studio or casting office the day before to pick up the script he has to learn.

14. If there are brothers or sisters in the family, are you prepared to deal with any sibling rivalry that may crop up?

At this point, you may be thinking you could never deal with these kinds of situations. Well, they are all just examples of situations that *could* occur. Any activity has its ups and downs, its good and bad days. To paraphrase an old saying: If it were a simple thing to do, with no problems, no hard work, and never the slightest disappointment, then *everyone* would be doing it.

And it's always a good idea to keep this in mind: It *is* a hot and cold business. There may be times when you and your child feel stretched to the limit; but just as quickly, things can come to a screeching halt. As a matter of fact, you will probably find yourself getting just as anxious when the phone doesn't ring.

The following are the most important points to remember:

1. Don't take the entertainment business too seriously. Think of it as a big game. There's always another

audition. Life will go on. You have everything to gain, and really nothing to lose.

2. Enjoy the experience and time spent with your child. Not everyone gets to do something as interesting as this.

3. One thing is absolutely certain—in this business as with any aspect of life: If you don't at least try, *nothing* will happen.

16

TALENT UNIONS

he following list of talent union offices can provide you with a current list of union-affiliated talent agents. Contact the nearest regional office for information regarding the location of a union office in your area.

Screen Actors Guild (SAG)

California

National Headquarters
7065 Hollywood Boulevard
Hollywood, CA 90028
(213) 465-4600

235 Pine Street, #1100
San Francisco, CA 94104
(415) 391-7510

Florida

2299 Douglas Road, #200
Miami, FL 33145
(305) 444-7677

Sun Bank Plaza, #302
3393 West Vine Street
Kissimee, FL 34741
(407) 847-4445

Illinois

307 North Michigan
Chicago, IL 60601
(312) 372-8081

Michigan

28690 Southfield Road
Lathrup Village, MI 48076
(313) 559-9540

New York

National Headquarters
1515 Broadway, 44th Floor
New York, NY 10036
(212) 944-1030

Texas

6309 North O'Connor Road
Irving, TX 75039
(214) 869-3556

2650 Fountainview, #326
Houston, TX 77057
(713) 972-1806

American Federation of Television and Radio Artists (AFTRA)

California

6922 Hollywood Boulevard,
8th Floor
Hollywood, CA 90028-6128
(213) 461-8111

235 Pine Street, #1100
San Francisco, CA 94104
(415) 391-7510

Florida

20401 N.W. Second Avenue,
#102
Miami, FL 33169
(305) 652-4824

Illinois

307 North Michigan Avenue
Chicago, IL 60601
(312) 372-8081

Michigan

28690 Southfield Road
Lathrup Village, MI 48076
(313) 559-9540

New York

260 Madison Avenue,
7th Floor
New York, NY 10016
(212) 532-0800

Texas

6060 North Central Expressway,
#302
Dallas, TX 75206
(214) 363-8300

2650 Fountainview, #326
Houston, TX 77057
(713) 972-1806

ABOUT THE AUTHOR

David Matis is the owner of Rising Stars, a personal management and talent development company located in Santa Monica, California. His clients have appeared in hundreds of commercials and in starring roles for television and feature films. He resides in Santa Monica with his wife, Joan. This is his second book.

INDEX